SAN FRANCISCO
CITY OF MANY DREAMS

First English edition published by Colour Library International Ltd.
© 1983 Illustrations and Text: Colour Library International Ltd.
    99 Park Avenue, New York, N.Y. 10016, U.S.A.
This edition published by Crescent Books
Distributed by Crown Publishers, Inc.
h g f e d c b a
Colour separations by FER-CROM, Barcelona, Spain.
Display and text filmsetting by ACESETTERS LTD., Richmond, Surrey, England.
Printed and bound in Barcelona, Spain by **Cayfosa,** and EUROBINDER.
ISBN 0-517-405482

Dep. Leg. B. 13.133/83

SAN FRANCISCO

CITY OF MANY DREAMS

Text by Joanne Dunn

Produced by
TED SMART and **DAVID GIBBON**

CRESCENT BOOKS

It couldn't have been anything else but a beautiful city. Not because the people who built it contrived to make it so; few cities were erected more heedlessly than this one. It is beautiful because the forces of earth, wind and water have provided it with a setting so splendid that man would need more time than he has had to overcome it.

The movement of the earth brought the hills of rock out of the sea, the water carried sand from the south and deposited it on the edge of the land. The winds, strong enough to blow sand over heights of six hundred feet, carried it into valleys between the hills making the hills less steep, more gently sloped. These are San Francisco's hills – Rincon Hill, Potrero Hill, Mt. Davidson, Twin Peaks, Lone Mountain. Not seven, as is sometimes said, but forty-three in all.

Of course this means that a fair number of the streets have to be climbed but it is always worth it. You will be rewarded for your trouble with a view of hills to the north and the south, and water to the east and west. There is nothing like standing on a hill looking down on or away from everyone else to help keep you from feeling hemmed in.

The water also forced its way through the low cliffs and flooded a river valley to make a bay as large as an inland sea, leaving the land surrounded on three sides by water. For five miles, the city shares a disputed border with the Pacific Ocean, as ill-chosen a name as ever there was. In the summer the ocean literally gives ground, depositing sand to build up the beach. In the winter, the ocean indulges in displays of power. The surf crashes in over rocks it has cut off from the coast and carries the sand away, sometimes as much as several feet in a day. There are small beaches inside the strait, such as the one known as Phelan Beach on the maps, and China Beach by people who know how to get to it, which may disappear completely after a stormy winter.

Ocean Beach is not much good for swimming. The water is cold – all the time – thanks to a current off the coast. Thanks to rip tides, the water is treacherous. The sea wall at Ocean Beach is posted with notices. These do not prohibit swimming; they merely provide you with the information that drownings occur every year. Believe these signs. Some of the people who drown are not swimmers but waders swept away by the currents. The only other signs in San Francisco you should pay so much attention to are those on certain streets advising motorists to set their brakes and curb their wheels. What Ocean Beach is good for is walking. On winter days you can sometimes have it almost to yourself. Nowhere else in San Francisco can you walk for five uninterrupted miles along flat ground.

What about swimming at the more protected beaches inside the strait? Not along the outer gate where the waves slow and break. A recent storm just washed away a hundred feet of wall and road there. Further inside the gate, Baker's Beach is better protected. Ships once anchored there to take on water from Lobos Creek. This beach is safer but not completely safe. You can swim in the bay at Aquatic Park but you may as well know that the bath houses built to accommodate the expected throngs of swimmers were turned into a museum for lack of custom. Accept the fact that most of the coast of Northern California is a wildly beautiful affair of cliffs, rock and crashing surf. If you want to bask in sun and sand you've come to the wrong place.

The climate is a perfect complement for the setting. For one thing, if there were snow the hills would become non-negotiable making most of the city uninhabitable in the winter. But it doesn't get cold enough to snow. The annual mean temperature is fifty-six degrees. In the coldest months, the mean temperature sinks to fifty degrees and shoots up to nearly sixty-two on the warmest days. The days are never hot; the nights are always cool.

Although San Francisco has sunshine sixty-six percent of the daylight hours, winter brings rain. This happens regularly every year. This does not stop many San Franciscans from greeting the rainy day with a mixture of disbelief and aggrievement. They expect good weather and can't be persuaded to take the broad view which included rain in this category. Even in the midst of a severe drought the best they would do was allow that it might not be a bad thing if perhaps there would be some rain in a little while, maybe tomorrow. If the possibility of rain must be considered in the winter, it can be ignored in the summer. You can plan an outdoor summertime event years in advance and know that on the day appointed there will be no rain.

Apart from the wet and the dry, San Francisco has no distinct seasons. They tend to be more subtle and less distinguishable from each other than those in some other places. They also tend not to follow the calendar faithfully. If your self-winding digital calendar watch stops, you might find your sense of time completely disrupted here. What does spring mean to a place with a year-round growing season, to which robins come to spend the winter? It starts with the new growth brought by the first rains in October and November then goes away and returns in the lengthening days of February and March when the acacias bloom. Cypress, eucalyptus and pine don't shed their leaves. September is the warmest month. Mark Twain once complained that the coldest winter he ever spent was a summer in San Francisco. He had reason.

The reason is the wind. The winds provide a variableness to the weather which might otherwise became tedious in a climate that is a model of moderation. Spring and summer bring the winds. They are pushed by the more or less permanent high pressure system that resides out over the water and pulled inland by the heat of the valleys. The more the summer sun heats the valleys, the stronger the winds that blow over San Francisco.

With the spring winds from the ocean comes fog. The city and the entrance to the bay form the only sea level break in the coastal mountain range. The golden gate is a gate that gives entry to the winds and the fog. Early in the season the fog collects in small patches and drifts in over the beach and around the hilltops. Later it masses off the coast and rolls in late in the day to spend the night and then burn off in the morning sun. The fog has its own daily and seasonal cycles and comes in many forms. It drifts in in wisps, streams in over the tops of the trees in Golden Gate Park; it may roll in over the water like a huge breaker or fall out of the sky. It may appear opaque above or below or beyond you but where you are it is transparent, a mist veiling distant things.

If you don't like the weather here, you're in luck. San Francisco's climate is pretty well restricted to the city itself. All you have to do to find something different is leave town. If you want an opportunity to wear all those hot weather clothes you have no use for here, cross a bridge. You'll notice a difference halfway across. All of California is somewhat warmer than places in the same latitude east of the mountains but the further you go from the coast, the more pronounced become the seasons. You can find snow for skiing in the mountains. The inland valleys offer anything you could want in the way of warmth. If not, you don't have to go very far to find desert. When you get too warm or too cold or too dry, come back.

San Francisco's climate and setting make her at once the "cool grey city of love" and a city of light. Light reflected from ocean swells, from the surrounding waters of the bay, from the leaves of eucalyptus trees, from fog and salt-bleached buildings. The eucalyptus trees were not part of the original package. For these, and the acacias, we are indebted to some unknown Australian who was kind enough to bring a tree to a gold rush. It was just what we needed. When walking through San Francisco remember that no forests were cleared to make room for it. Every tree you see was planted. One of the first people to explore what is now the city wrote in his diary that there was not a tree in sight. The building of a park was discouraged by people who felt that the land could not support even one full-sized tree. Even the redwoods which grow for hundreds of miles along the coast did not grow here. Today there is eucalyptus everywhere. Adolph Sutro, one of early San Francisco's leading citizens, planted them by the thousands and gave thousands more away to children to plant for arbor day. They adapted so well to this climate that they were planted in large numbers in Golden Gate Park. The one thing largely responsible for the proliferation of these trees was a sort of get-rich-eventually scheme which was supposed to be the answer to a hardwood shortage. All the smart entrepreneur had to do was buy land planted with eucalyptus trees, watch them grow and, in ten years time, reap his profit. Huge amounts of empty land were planted for this purpose until someone discovered that there are at least six hundred varieties of eucalyptus and that the variety planted here was useless as a source of hardwood.

The varieties grown for hardwood in Australia take about one hundred years to reach the felling stage. This was a little too long-range even for the more patient types and they went on to other speculations leaving forests behind where none had been before.

There is, really, only one imperfection which consists of several faults. Actually, several major and numerous minor faults which nature has provided in case she wants to improve on her handiwork or simply rearrange things. The ever-present prospect of seismic activity must be considered an undesirable feature. We welcome the movement of the wind and water which contribute so much to our days but continuing movement of the earth is something else. There are better things for a city to be than geologically interesting.

San Francisco is not a large city. It covers only 44.6 square miles not including the Farallone Islands. The Farallones, a chain of islands thirty miles off the coast, became part of the City and County of San Francisco in 1872. Drake landed on one of these islands after leaving what he had called New Albion and he named them the Islands of St. James. No one paid any attention, however, since they were among the few places in the whole California territory which already had a name. They had long been known to navigators plying the trade route between Mexico and the Philippines. Other passing ships gave various names to the stretch of water between the islands and the coast but it is still known as the Gulf of the Farallones. The islands are now a wildlife sanctuary and are not open to the public.

The Farallones together with Yerba Buena Island, Alcatraz and Angel Island in the bay and a large portion of the present city, were claimed by a Frenchman in the 1840s. He said the land had been granted to him by a governor of Mexico to whom he had given a loan of $4,000. If so, this would have been a bargain second only to that made for Manhattan. It was generally agreed that Angel Island belonged to a man named Osio, it having been granted to him by another (or the same) governor in 1839. The United States government spent a great deal of money contesting the claim. When the claim was defeated, title reverted to Mexico from which the United States later purchased Yerba Buena Island. The government obtained Angel Island by executive order which was probably much cheaper than a lawsuit.

All the islands in San Francisco Bay have been under the command of the military. Alcatraz, the name is Spanish for pelican, was used as a military prison from the Civil War through World War I. In 1934 the Justice Department acquired it for a maximum-security penitentiary. The "rock" achieved such a grim reputation as a penal institution that agitation to have it closed down began two years later. It didn't close until 1963 when it became too expensive to keep up. Subsequently, Alcatraz Island was twice occupied by Indian groups who cited a treaty giving Indians the right to unoccupied federal land which Alcatraz certainly was. The government resisted, possibly on principle, possibly to avoid setting the precedent of honoring an Indian treaty. Being well aware of all the charms of the island, they adopted the strategy of outwaiting the occupiers. It nearly worked but at the end of two years their resolution gave out and the remaining ten adults and five children were removed by force. The popular feeling towards the place was best expressed by Frank Weatherman, one of the last prisoners to leave Alcatraz who opined that "Alcatraz never was no good for nobody." Today it is included in the park system and guided tours have been given since 1973. These tours are extremely popular and usually require advance reservations. The boat ride out is fine.

Angel Island was also used as an internment facility. It is now a federal game refuge and a perfect place to spend the day hiking and picnicking. Yerba Buena Island was used as a naval training station.

Treasure Island is a man-made addition dredged up from the bay to serve as the site of the Golden Gate International Exposition of 1939. The exposition was a celebration of the completion of the San Francisco-Oakland Bay Bridge and the Golden Gate Bridge. Work began in 1936 and continued for eighteen months resulting in a four-hundred acre island. It was built over some shoals which were considered to be a navigational nuisance. A nine-hundred foot causeway was built to the island. Trees were hauled in by barge and planted along with hundreds of thousands of flowers. The ongoing festival continued for a year. The truly unique thing about the construction of Treasure Island is that it was completed at slightly less than its estimated cost. This island belongs to the City of San Francisco but is leased by the Navy.

Laying out a city on hills involves solving some special problems and the solutions sometimes produce some interesting effects; steps occasionally merge with level ground, windows and doors are asymmetrical and buildings meet the ground at odd angles. No great thought was given to the hills when the streets were laid out. Streets just went on doggedly following a simple grid pattern come what may. Hills may arise in the center of a block. Lombard Street solved the problem of a too precipitous incline by having eight curves in a one-block stretch thereby earning itself postcard status and billing as the crookedest street in the world. Vermont solved a similar problem the same way but since it has only six turns, it places a distant second and has a smaller following. In other places, streets simply went through the hills instead of over them. In a few places the towel had to be thrown in and a street will come to an abrupt end at the base of an escarpment.

Street names are one place where San Francisco's history is preserved. Nearly all of the people who contributed to the discovery, growth and events of San Francisco have streets named for them. At least one fellow achieved this distinction by coming up with the price of a bottle of champagne when it was particularly wanted. Other streets commemorate people for reasons known only to the people who named them.

One of the men responsible for the naming of some of the streets was called Gough. He named one street after his sister, Octavia, and one after himself, Gough Street. Somebody must once have known how to pronounce this name but no longer. Have you ever considered the possibilities offered by the spelling, g-o-u-g-h? The most common renditions are go, goff, and gow but there is no reason why you shouldn't select any other which you might prefer. Many names have been changed over the years for various reasons. I believe Rattlesnake Street was discarded early on. Unfortunately, Gough Street was not one of those to be changed.

If you thought the grid pattern of streets was unimaginative, what will you think of the fact that numbers were used twice. The numbered streets are located south of Market Street. Numbered avenues are in the western part of the city. If you mean "avenue" you have to specify avenue. If you just say 10th or 17th, you are talking about the street. There is a 13th St.

but no 13th Ave. However, at the corner of Geary Blvd. and what would have been 13th Avenue, the word "thirteenth" is written in the cement where the names of the streets are located. Either the name was changed or a worker charged with engraving the names became mesmerized with the monotony of the thing and let logic take its course. I always considered the practice of writing street names in the sidewalk cement a good one even though the children here do not appear to be sufficiently dull-witted to spend their time removing street signs as they are known to do in other places.

For a way, you can easily find your way across the Sunset district where the streets running at right angles to the numbered avenues are in alphabetical order. This system begins with J and ends with W leaving us without a Xanthippe Street.

There are two major exceptions to the grid pattern. Columbus Avenue cuts a diagonal from a point near Portsmouth Square to a point near Fishermans' Wharf. The other exception is Market Street which was laid out along the original path from the bay to the Mission Dolores. It no doubt seemed like a good idea at the time. It seemed less of a good idea when the streets laid out on the square intersected at Market Street at curious angles leaving small triangular islands in the middle of preposterous intersections. Known as the "slot," Market Street became a line of demarcation separating the area of fashionable hotels and fine houses north of it from the industrial area to the south.

San Francisco Bay is considered to be one of the safest harbors in the world. There are some fairly dangerous areas to be negotiated at the entrance such as the bit of turbulent water off the north head of the strait called the Potato Patch and the sometimes shallow water over the Great Bar. There is also a system of fog horns, lights, buoys, bells and whistles to guide ships through the deepened main channel. Before this system was available, the fogs and submerged rocks and shoals in the gulf outside the strait made for a forbidding coastline which discouraged navigators from close investigation.

For this reason, the natural land-locked harbor went undiscovered despite exploration of the Pacific coast specifically for the purpose of locating a safe harbor for vessels engaged in trade between Mexico and the Far East. Among the first known to have overlooked it were Fortuno Ximenes and Juan Cabrillo who sailed past it in 1534 and 1542 respectively. Bartolome Ferrelo followed the coast as far as Oregon without sighting it. The most famous seafarer to preserve the bay's status as an unknown was Sir Francis Drake who, in 1579, discovered Drake's Bay instead, while looking for a place to prepare his ship for a Pacific crossing. He named the land New Albion and claimed it in the name of Queen Elizabeth. He is also said to have placed a brass plate testifying to that effect somewhere about the place. In 1933 a brass plate was discovered near a ranch on the eastern shore of the bay. The plate occasioned much controversy before a concensus was reached that it was genuine and it was put on display in the Bancroft Library on the University of California campus in Berkeley. Drake's Bay was later rediscovered by Sebastian Cermeño who renamed it in honor of St. Francis of Assisi. Since that name was subsequently pinched by its neighbor to the south, Drake still has his namesake. That bay was not considered to have met the specification of a safe harbor after Cermeño's ship was wrecked there during a storm. The survivors had to sail home in the ship's launch and Cermeño later died from complications from a broken arm he had suffered there. Seven years later, Monterey Bay was discovered and everyone promptly forgot about the whole thing for the next 150 years or so. Ximenes, Cabrillo and Drake were to be memorialized by the placing of a bronze sundial dedicated to them in Golden Gate Park, although it is a little difficult to say just why.

In the 1700s Alta California again became of interest to the Spanish. (At the time, California had no precise geographical definition. The name, taken from an old Spanish story, was given to what is now Baja or Lower California. Everything north of that, whatever it may chance to be, was referred to as Alta or Upper California.) The Spanish realized that, more than being useful as a place for ships to take on water and make repairs, Alta California was necessary to defend New Spain against encroachments from other European powers. California would have to be colonized.

The method employed was to send out small groups of priests and soldiers with a few settlers to establish a string of missions, each protected by a garrison, along the coast. The first of these was located at San Diego and from there they were located at intervals northward. In the end then, San Francisco was not discovered from the sea at all but by a land party; one of several who were trying to find Monterey Bay to establish a mission there.

The first party to start up the peninsula sighted the gulf of the Farallones and, realizing they had missed Monterey, turned back. The leader of the party which first came upon the strait leading from the ocean to the bay realized only that this stretch of water prevented him from going even further out of his way than he had already gone and returned, disgruntled, with his tale of woe.

In 1775, Lt. Manuel de Ayala sailed his ship, the San Carlos, into San Francisco Bay. He spent a week there and was able to report that this bay, with 236 miles of coastline, would indeed make a satisfactory port. On his second trip one year later, Ayala was met by a small group of settlers who had made the trek overland with one platoon of soldiers and two priests.

By September of 1776, the presidio, the military garrison and the mission were established. The mission was dedicated to St. Francis but became known as the Mission Dolores after a nearby lake which the priests called La Laguna de los Dolores, the lake of sorrows. This turns out not to have been because the padres were discouraged by the hardships of their journey but only that it was the Friday before Palm Sunday, "sorrowful Friday" in the church calendar.

The small settlement did not prosper. The soldiers, finding nothing to defend against, made no attempt to keep up the fortifications. It would have been difficult in any case. Supply ships were few and far between and eventually stopped coming altogether. The people at the presidio became entirely dependent upon the mission for food and clothing. The mission was supported by the labor of the Indian converts who kept sheep and cattle, made furniture and raised food for the small community. The most lucrative enterprise was a hide and tallow trade which became a thriving industry and which attracted ships to the bay. The other attraction of San Francisco Bay was the fact that customs' duties were seldom collected there. The soldiers, whose responsibility this was, were not inclined to deprive themselves of the few luxuries and the only companionship which offered itself. Besides, Mexico City was a long way away. News of the Mexican revolution in 1821 was a long time in coming and was received with equanimity. When, in 1825, they learned that they were now part of the Republic of Mexico, a mass was said, the working cannon at the presidio were fired, and everyone went back to the business of amusing themselves as best they could.

In time, many of the Indians tired of the novelty of laboring at the mission and went back to their villages while others wintered there but left in the summer. Others responded to the blessings of civilization by developing smallpox and tuberculosis. It was becoming obvious that there was a limit to the amount of food and the number of grazing animals that could be raised on sandy hillsides. So, to improve the health of the Indians, to look for lusher ground, and perhaps because the Mexican government was not sanguine about the activities of the Russian hunting colony established to the north at Fort Ross, most of the inhabitants of the mission left to found another mission at Sonoma.

Secularization of the missions began in 1834. Part of the land was to be reserved for the support of the priests and the rest was to be divided among the Indians. It wasn't, of course. Most of the land was absorbed by the ranchos. These were holdings of Spanish families given land grants so they would live in upper California and represent the interests of the government. Many of them were extensive. The Rancho San Antonio consisted of 48,000 acres and is now the site of several cities in the east bay. General Mariano Guadalupe Vallejo's Petaluma rancho was substantially larger.

By the time Mexico became concerned about maintaining supremacy in California, it was too late. With the loss of the missions, the presidio had fallen nearly to ruin. The few remaining soldiers had been there for six or seven years without pay. They felt no great loyalty to Mexico. The Russians were proving difficult to evict from Fort Ross and representatives of the Hudson Bay Company did not fail to notice the inadequacy of the defenses at the presidio. The first permanent house had been built in 1835 and a pueblo or town had grown up around the cove where the ships anchored. The cove and the pueblo were called Yerba Buena, Spanish for "good herb," after an aromatic plant that grew

there. At first, foreigners had been welcomed. That was because most of them came by ship, married into local families and became Mexican citizens. Some of them, like the Swiss, John Sutter, had been given land grants. A later group were not so well-received. It consisted largely of hunters and trappers who came over the mountains, stayed in the interior, and scorned any attempts to dislodge them. The original Spanish families, so long cut off from Mexico, began to think of themselves as Californios, Californians, and talked of a republic independent of Mexico – the only point of contention being who was to lead it. Four Governors were driven out of Monterey. The last of these was Governor Manuel Micheltorena. He was forced to leave after the battle of Cahuenga Pass in which a horse was killed on one side and a mule wounded on the other. This was one of the first pitched battles in the epic struggle for power in California.

1841, the year the first actual settler came over the mountains, was also the year it became illegal to engage in any foreign trade in California. In 1845 a ban on further American immigration was imposed. By that time there were already more Americans than Californios in California. Relations between Mexico and the United States had been poor since 1835 when President Andrew Jackson (he of Manifest Destiny fame) tried to purchase all of Northern California. He wanted San Francisco Bay as a port for Pacific whaling ships. Also, he disliked the idea of a foreign country being in control of what he considered to be the natural western boundary of the United States. Things did not improve when Jackson "annexed" Texas the following year.

Then there occurred one of those little misunderstandings that will take place from time to time. Commodore Thomas Catesby Jones, under the impression that the U.S. was at war with Mexico and believing that the British were sending a force against Monterey, sailed to Monterey and demanded that the garrison there surrender. The garrison, 29 soldiers, a few militia and little ammunition, did so. Jones raised the American flag and was in the process of taking over all aspects of government when he discovered that he had made a mistake. He lowered the flag, apologized handsomely to the Mexican officials, and sailed away.

In spite of the ban on American immigration, a United States army topographer named John Fremont was allowed to remain with his 60 armed men after agreeing to keep to his stated purpose of surveying his way north to Oregon. He didn't. He eventually made his way to Sonoma where, with his encouragement but not his active participation, some of the local Americans engaged in incidents with the Californios. These incidents led to an unofficial American uprising when a group of these, variously estimated at from 17 to 33, appeared at General Vallejo's home and demanded the surrender of the pueblo of Sonoma. Vallejo, somewhat puzzled by the appearance of the group whom he described as being dressed in coyote skins, was nevertheless hospitable. He invited a deputation inside to discuss the matter over brandy. The discussion was surely just getting interesting when some of the men grew restive at the amount of time the proceedings were taking and went inside to see how the surrender was progressing. They had the general taken and imprisoned at Sutter's Fort. The flag of Mexico was hauled down and was replaced by a hastily-devised banner with a star, a red bar and a grizzly bear drawn on it. The banner, with some improvements in the artistic execution, became the state flag of California. It was never clear whether Fremont was acting on his own initiative or not but it is pretty well agreed that the whole affair was pointless and harmful. Harmful because many of the Californios including General Vallejo, had favored union with the United States and were put off by this incident. Pointless because at the time the incident took place, the United States was at war with Mexico.

The village of Yerba Buena became American territory on July 9, 1846 when Commander John Montgomery sailed the Portsmouth into Yerba Buena cove and raised the flag over what is now Portsmouth Square. Finding no Mexican officials in Yerba Buena, Montgomery directed that the flag be raised at all other settlements in the north where, according to Soule's Annals of California, "it was received with tranquility if not applause." Later, General S. W. Kearney issued a proclamation. It was a chatty affair explaining that Mexico had forced war on the United States so fast that there just wasn't time to invite its good friends in California to join them in a neighborly way and that it had therefore been necessary to occupy the land in order to prevent its being grabbed by a European power.

Alta California was officially ceded to the United States by the treaty of Guadalupe Hidalgo on Feb. 2, 1848, just nine days after gold flakes were found in the mill race at Sutter's mill. Had gold been discovered years earlier, the history of California would have been significantly different.

Sam Brannan came to Yerba Buena in 1846 intending to establish a Mormon settlement. He brought with him 200 settlers thereby doubling the pueblo's population. When he had left the east coast, California still belonged to Mexico. Brannan was disconcerted to find the American flag in Portsmouth Square. Some said this was because he had wanted to be the first to raise the flag himself. Others claimed that Brannan had wanted to settle outside of U.S. jurisdiction and was annoyed at finding "that damn rag" in his new home. In either case, the settlers remained and published Yerba Buena's first newspaper, the California Star. In January of 1847 the Star announced the renaming of Yerba Buena to San Francisco, an announcement that had little or no impact on the inhabitants. He was far more successful with his second scoop, however. It was Sam Brannan who rode through Portsmouth Square in January of 1848 waving a bottle of gold flakes crying the discovery of gold on the American River. This item had the effect of emptying the whole town in a matter of hours. It may or may not be true that this particular bit of news was delayed until Brannan, who owned a store at Sutter's fort, was able to stock his store with an ample supply of the sort of thing a person likes to have when he has decided to go prospecting for gold.

Considering how long it had always taken for news to get to San Francisco, the word of the gold strike got out quickly enough. A newspaper article chronicling the growth of the town noted that in 1844 there were 12 houses and fewer than 50 people but that by 1848 San Francisco had 135 finished dwellings, 10 unfinished dwellings, 12 stores and warehouses, 35 shanties and a school. By January 1849 there were 6,000 people in the goldfields and 2,000 people to occupy those 193 buildings in San Francisco. Between 1847 and 1848, only four ships had arrived in the harbor.

In the twelve months after word of the gold discovery reached the east coast, 777 ships sailed for San Francisco. The first steamship arrived in February 1849 overloaded with goldseekers from Chile, Peru and Mexico and some from New Orleans who had crossed Panama to meet it. The ship was immediately deserted by crew and passengers alike. In the following months hundreds of vessels would be left abandoned and rotting in the harbor as crews deserted to seek their fortunes. By 1850 San Francisco had a population of 50,000, most of them living in tents or whatever shelters could be hastily erected.

The question arises, Why San Francisco? The goldfields were located a hundred miles inland and could only be reached by crossing the bay or by treking down the peninsula and back up the eastern shore of the bay. Surely an anchorage could have been found on that eastern shore which would have been a more convenient jumping off place for the argonauts as they came to be called. It didn't happen that way. San Francisco's population had grown to 56,800 people in 1860 while that of Oakland, directly across the way, was only 1,500. It seems that even then there was something special about this place.

As San Francisco became more and more built up and people began to realize that here was going to be a permanent city with permanent residents, more attention was paid to means of making it more habitable. There was a demand for land to be set aside as a public park. Frederick Law Olmsted, designer of New York's Central Park was invited to San Francisco to give his advice as to the best place for such a park. Olmsted advised that the low-lying area along Van Ness Avenue be landscaped and planted with flowers and shrubs, that other sunken parkways be made and that a 120-acre park be created in the lee of one of the hills. His advice was not taken. San Francisco didn't want promenades. It wanted a park, a large park, a park even bigger than New York City's. The area finally selected had nothing whatsoever to recommend it as a park site except its size and the fact that it was cheap since no one wanted it for anything else. The chosen site was a strip about three miles long and one-half mile wide running from the ocean towards the city. The western part of it consisted of sand dunes whose contours changed constantly in the winds blowing from the ocean. The eastern section was a mixture of clay and rock with the emphasis on the latter. Its vegetation consisted almost entirely of the wild strawberry plants which had managed to find a purchase on the protected side of a small hill. Unpromising as it was, there really weren't many other areas in San Francisco which were any better suited to the project.

The contract for developing the park was given to an engineer named William Hammond Hall. Hall had the advantage of being familiar with the empty western portion of the peninsula since he had made maps of it for the Army. He also had the distinction of believing that the area could be transformed into a park, a matter in which his was the minority opinion. The majority either laughed at the city's 1,015-acre white elephant or lamented that this folly would prove a very expensive one indeed.

Hall's first problem was solved by tapping underground streams which he found to be close beneath the surface. Water would not be a difficulty. The difficulty was in finding a plant, any plant, that would consent to grow in a wind-swept patch of constantly shifting sand. He learned that the traditional method of overcoming similar problems was the use of cut brush to protect the plants while they took root, but San Francisco didn't have much to offer in the brush line. Hall finally discovered that barley would grow in the sand and hold it until native lupine could take root. In 1870 he began planting trees. Monterey pine, eucalyptus and cypress. By 1876 most of the park was planted with trees and people were using it for outings. The park was widely praised as a remarkable accomplishment. At about this time however, Hall's troubles began in earnest. For the preceding six years, Hall had been fighting off politicians and promoters who threatened the integrity of his park. He had also managed to alienate two factions; one of which wanted all the elevations levelled so that formal gardens could be laid out and the other wanted no tampering whatsoever with the original topography. Formal gardens were not at all Hall's idea of a park but neither did he hesitate to create lakes and use the earth to form meadows. Hall's many enemies eventually succeeded in having the budget for the park cut so severely that he resigned rather than try to carry on under impossible conditions. The next ten years were years of decline under a succession of managers. Deterioration due to neglect was so extensive that Frederick Olmsted became alarmed and wrote to influential people in San Francisco asking them to do something to keep the park from falling into total ruin. Hall was called back and, because he was unable to devote his full time to the park, he chose a supervisor, John McClaren, to work with him. When an old political enemy of Hall's was made park commissioner in 1889, Hall again quit leaving the park to McClaren who was to remain as superintendent until his death in 1943 at the age of 96.

Like Hall, McClaren preferred trees, flowers and lawns to tennis courts and buildings. Unlike Hall, he was willing to accept things he didn't want in order to get the money for the things he did want. He planted redwood trees and hybrid flowers. He imported his favorites, rhododendrons, from all over the world. Only in England's Kew Gardens were there more varieties and even there there were fewer specimens. He created the Shakespeare Garden containing every flower and plant mentioned in the plays. Private gifts to the park enabled McClaren to build a children's playground. Others provided a music temple and the Hall of Flowers. The Stybring Arboretum contains over 5,000 species of plants and trees arranged in geographical groupings.

Harder for McClaren to accept were the many monuments and statues donated to the park. He hated them but he couldn't keep them out. Instead, he planted shrubbery and vines to obscure them. It was some time after his death that the offending flora were finally dug out. After his death, a statue of McClaren was erected in the Golden Gate Park. Even this, however, was not the final irony. In his honor, a rhododendron dell was planted and, in order to protect the new plants, in that spot was placed the one thing John McClaren hated even more than statues: a "Keep Off the Grass" sign.

In the winter of 1894/95 a mid-winter festival was held at the suggestion of M. H. de Young who felt it might help revive a slumping economy. In five months over 100 buildings were erected in the park. One of these was a fine arts building and de Young himself went to Europe to collect objects for exhibition. The festival was a success and de Young asked that excess profits be used to accumulate a permanent art collection. The temporary building was torn down and the M. H. de Young Museum of Art moved into its permanent home in 1917. Wings were added in 1925 and 1931. One wing now houses the Asian Art Museum centered around a collection offered to the city by Avery Brundage. The museum also offers educational exhibits, art classes and an art reference library. Across the music concourse, also built for the festival, is the California Academy of Science, the Steinhart

Aquarium and the Morrison Planetarium.

One of the most popular attractions in Golden Gate Park was another exhibit erected for the mid-winter fair. This is the Japanese Tea Garden; a five-acre garden of Japanese maples, magnolia trees, camellias and other plants set among pools, bridges and bamboo-railed walks. It was originally begun by an Australian but then came under the care of the Hagiwara family who eventually moved into the garden, tended it and improved it for three generations. In 1942 the family was expelled from its garden and interned with other Americans of Japanese ancestry. Only this year has a bill been introduced before the San Francisco Board of Supervisors calling for some compensation, however token it must be, to the three surviving members of the Hagiwara family.

When Olmsted first made his recommendations for a park he urged that it should be a pleasure spot not only for the present population but for future generations and millions of others as well. Golden Gate Park is all of that. It is a haven for walkers, joggers, roller skaters, bicyclists, museum goers, frisbee players, picknickers, and several buffalo. Sunday, when the park is closed to traffic, is a favorite day for coming to the park. If you don't like crowds, there are always places where you can take a solitary ramble, especially in the western end of the park where you can end your walk at the ocean.

When Father Junipero Serra arrived in San Francisco before it was San Francisco or even before it Yerba Buena, he believed that he had reached the end of California. He observed that from there it was only possible to go forward by boat. From his point of view, the tip of the peninsula, he was correct. He hadn't thought of bridges. San Francisco Bay has five bridges, six if you count the Carquinez bridge linking San Pablo Bay with Suisun Bay.

The first of these was the Dumbarton Bridge, built in 1927 to span the bay at its narrowest point. In 1929, the San Mateo Bridge joined San Mateo and Alameda counties across 7 miles of water in the south bay. 1936 saw the opening of the San Francisco-Oakland Bay Bridge, a double span bridge whose east and west crossings are connected by a 4-story high tunnel on Yerba Buena island. Six months after the opening of the Bay Bridge, the Golden Gate Bridge was completed. It was not the first nor the longest but it is the best loved, it is THE bridge. It is certainly the most beautiful and has the advantage of the best setting. It hangs over the strait between the ocean and the bay as if it had been spun there.

Joseph Strauss first suggested that a bridge across the strait be built in 1918. The idea took some time to catch on and approval was not given until 1930. Construction did not begin until 1932. Construction of the north tower at Lime Point in Marin County was relatively simple but the building of the south tower required greater ingenuity. The foundation had to be placed on a rock shelf some distance out in the water. Initially, work could only be done between the tides. Then workers tried working from a floating platform that rose and fell with swells up to 15 feet. This was difficult and became impossible when the platform was rammed and sunk by a freighter. A concrete barrier 30 inches thick was erected but even that was smashed in a collision with a caisson which was being positioned when a storm blew up. It was finally necessary to build a complete concrete enclosure and pump out the water in order to lay the foundation.

Strauss' safety record was impressive. He had a safety net erected at a cost estimated at between 80 and 150 thousand dollars. The expense was justified in the minds of the "To Hell and Back" club formed by the men who fell and were saved by the net. There are 19 recorded instances of lives being saved but the actual number was probably higher.

When the towers were completed, the cables were strung. These, which appear so fragile from a distance, are 36 inches in diameter, composed of thousands of strands of thin wire. The bridge was built to withstand the severe winds that blow through the Golden Gate and has had to close only once in an exceptionally bad storm. The center span lies 220 feet above high water. Contrary to the expectations of some of the bridge's opponents, there has never been a problem of interference by the bridge with ships entering the bay. The only bad moment was during World War II when the Cunard liner Queen Elizabeth sailed in for a visit and cleared the bridge by an anxiety-producing small number of feet.

One unfortunate attraction the Golden Gate Bridge has is for suicides. More than 600 people have jumped to their deaths from the bridge and many others have been rescued. Toll booths contain closed-circuit television cameras which allow officials to view the entire length of the bridge. Local folklore has it that most suicides jump from the east side so they can have a last view of the city. It is more likely that the east side is chosen because that is where a person coming by car from San Francisco would wind up. And that is how most of them come, by car. Statistics show most come on a Tuesday, in May or October. Patrols on the bridge are increased whenever a new hundred mark approaches as it seems some distinction is felt to be achieved through being number 400 or 500. The question has arisen, and will arise again, of placing suicide barriers on the bridge. The objections are based less on cost or lack of practical effectiveness than on aesthetics: suicide barriers would spoil the appearance of the bridge. The same objection was once urged against the building of the bridge itself by people who felt that it would mar the beauty of what the Indians called the sunset strait. The military objected to it fearing that an enemy could destroy the bridge and leave the wreckage across the channel trapping the fleet inside. One hopes it was for a different reason that the fleet was later moved to Pearl Harbor.

When the Bay bridge opened, a three-day party was held with a parade, a regatta and fireworks. The Golden Gate bridge opened to an even bigger celebration. Californian poppies were planted at both approaches, schools were closed, a parade of ships passed under the bridge while 500 planes flew overhead. 250,000 people came to walk across the new bridge. All of Canada and Mexico were invited to the festivities. It had already been decided to hold an international gala to celebrate completion of the two bridges. It was held in 1939 on an island created for the purpose and went on for a year. San Francisco always did know how to throw a party.

When the sixth bridge, the Richmond – San Rafael, was completed in 1956, San Francisco Bay had 4 of the 10 largest bridges in the world.

Those who believed that the coming of the bridges would mean the end of the ferry boats were right. There had been a ferry service between San Francisco and the east bay since gold rush days. The priests at the Mission Dolores had once acquired two ships to act as a link between the missions. These were crewed and maintained by the Indians who had previously taken to the water only in reed canoes. The two small vessels were left to deteriorate. When a demand for them arose, a deal was quickly struck. The Kangaroo Line provided the first regular ferry service in 1850.

The last ferry made the trip to Oakland in 1958. The municipal band played a dirge while a white model of the boat was sunk. The Sausalito and Larkspur ferries still run to Marin County and commuters find it preferable to sitting in stalled traffic on a bridge. At present, both the bridges to San Francisco are thought to be inadequate. Perhaps it is time to bring back the ferries.

The Bay Bridge would be hopelessly inadequate if it were not augmented by BART, Bay Area Rapid Transit. This system was many years in planning. Even so, the first train was five years behind schedule and the cost was nearly twice what was estimated. The long-awaited trains were not an outstanding success. Planners had overlooked the fact that the brakes on this particular model did not work well on wet tracks. Outside of the city, most of the track is aboveground. The trains could not be made to appear at the promised intervals. The original plan called for such frequent service that no provision was made for straphangers of which there weren't expected to be any. Commuters who have never seen a seat on a BART train are hard put to find handholds. The blame was laid at the figurative feet of the computer, that universal scapegoat of the modern world. We are told it is antiquated. We are not told why we were provided with a system designed to be controlled entirely by computer, but without a computer capable of controlling it. Initially, service was so poor that the management had to provide a free-ride day to keep the peace. If you avoid rush hour (and it doesn't bother you to realize that you're travelling through a tube at the bottom of the bay), BART is clean, quiet, comfortable and convenient which are things people in American cities have learned not to expect from mass transit.

If the Golden Gate Bridge is identified with San Francisco, so are the cable cars. We owe the existence of this cheerful form of transportation to Andrew Hallidie. He set about inventing a method of transporting passengers up hills after witnessing an accident in which a horse was killed when the wagon it was hauling lost its brakes and rolled downhill. Hallidie got the idea for the cable cars from cars he had seen used in British coal mines. He invented a gripping device by which a car could attach itself to an underground cable moved by turning wheels. The 14-foot high wheels move the cable at a constant speed of nine miles per hour. This does not sound like much in these days of supersonic transport but it was faster than the horses it was designed to replace. I suspect that modern buses do not, all things considered, make much better time through the traffic of crowded city streets.

The first line, on Clay Street, carried passengers only six short blocks, to an elevation of 307 feet. Hallidie was sufficiently sanguine to be a passenger on the first downhill run. Soon many different lines ran for comparatively short distances over various routes. At one time there were about 600 cars gliding along 110 miles of track. Many of the cars and much of the track were destroyed in 1906 and they never came back in force. They were replaced by electric trolley cars and buses until they were reduced to fewer than 50 cars decorating 17 miles of track over three routes. It eventually became clear that the system was suffering from old age and that soon the sound of the cable car bell would no longer be heard in the land. In 1955 San Franciscans did a not-unexpected thing. They came to the defense of an endangered species. An amendment was added to the city charter providing for the maintenance and perpetuation of the cable cars. To repeal the amendment and abandon the cable cars would require a majority vote from the citizens of San Francisco. This is not likely, especially since the cars were given landmark status in 1964.

The cable cars are immensely popular and decidedly unprofitable. It soon became apparent that they were also increasingly unsafe. Operating the cars at a loss was one thing; paying out additional sums each year for the settlement of personal injury claims was quite another. One of these was a claim made by a woman who proved to the court's satisfaction that she had become a nymphomaniac as a result of a cable car accident. The safety record of the cable cars might have been improved if passengers were required to ride inside the car rather than clinging onto the outside but it is generally agreed that such a ride would be no ride at all. It was decided that either the cars would have to be scrapped or the machinery would have to be renovated. For the first time since 1873, there are no cable cars on San Francisco streets. But this is a temporary state of affairs. They are being repaired and restored, partly with money raised privately. Even those who have little occasion to ride them are glad that they can visit the cable car museum to see the first cable car but not the last.

April 18, 1906. Every year there are fewer people who witnessed the events of that day but it is no nearer being forgotten for all of that. That was the day when, in less than one minute in the early morning, the continuity of San Francisco was broken and everything that had occurred in the city up to that time became "before" for ever.

Many people had gone to bed late the night before after hearing Enrico Caruso sing in Carmen to a full house. This was the last time the city was to hear the master since Caruso never again appeared in San Francisco.

The reactions of the people wakened by the earth's restlessness varied according to the severity of the effect on their portion of the city. Some came out into streets that showed few signs of damage. Others were unable to estimate the extent of the destruction. Many remembered that Mt. Vesuvius had erupted not long before and decided they were part of a worldwide cataclysm. Rumors flew – the entire Pacific coast was in ruins, Chicago had been destroyed, the Atlantic coast had been inundated by a tidal wave. Those who lived in the neighborhoods south of Market Street whose small houses bore the brunt of the tremor came out into the middle of the streets, away from the buildings and stood still, in absolute silence, waiting.

What came was fire. Numerous small fires from toppled stoves erupted in the city 90 percent of whose houses were made of wood. The first discovery made by the firefighters was that the fire chief had been critically injured in the collapse of the fire station in which he slept. He died several days later without knowing what the fire had done. The second discovery was that the fire alarms weren't working; the third that all the water mains had been ruptured. The largest of these was found to have been laid directly along the San Andreas fault for a distance of seven miles. The others had burst where they had been placed in soft ground. A few buildings had their own water supply. Others were situated so that water could be pumped to them from the bay. For the rest there was nothing to be done. The only weapon against

the fire was dynamite to blow up buildings and try to stop the spread of the flames. A few of the structures which had been built to withstand fire, also withstood dynamite and had to be left standing. One of these was the Palace Hotel. It had water tanks on the roof and a reservoir in the basement but this was not enough for the eight hundred rooms and the interior was gutted.

The offices of the four newspapers lay in the fire's path and there was no power to run the presses. Facilities were borrowed from the Oakland Tribune (Oakland received no damage during the earthquake) and a joint effort edition was issued which contained no good news. While it was able to provide some accurate information and squelch some of the wilder rumors, it was far from reassuring: "Fire and Earthquake, San Francisco in ruins, death and destruction have been the city's fate." The ferries continued to run throughout for those who could reach them and thousands of people left the city by that route. A photograph taken from one of the boats on April 18, 1906 shows the ferry building and a wall of swirling smoke where a skyline should have been. Many left but more remained. Homeless, they streamed with such possessions as they thought to carry to the city's parks and any unscorched piece of ground they could find. San Francisco again became a city of tents. People who still had homes were forbidden to cook in them. Meals were prepared in the streets on fireplaces made from the plentiful supply of bricks from fallen chimneys.

Without being officially proclaimed, martial law went into effect. The soldiers were placed under the authority of the police and the mayor gave orders that looters were to be shot on sight. There was not much looting but at least one person was shot to death while trying to remove belongings from his own house. Police and soldiers with bayonets were uncompromising about clearing people from critical areas. One of the reasons, of course, was to protect them from the fire and the dynamite blasts. Another was that people had not been told that their homes were going to be blown up and no one was particularly eager to engage in confrontation with owners who might take exception.

A committee of 50 was appointed to help establish some order and, all in all, they were surprisingly effective. A holiday had to be declared to prevent a run on banks for money lying in steel vaults too hot to touch. Vehicles were commandeered and were used to carry orders throughout the city. Directives were written on walls and sidewalks or on planks nailed to buildings. Some of these carried the succinct admonition, "obey or get shot." There was, perhaps, no time for niceties. Sewer lines had been opened and there were fears of an epidemic. The wholesale food warehouses were all located in the part of the city which was the first to burn. By the time it occurred to the authorities to requisition the stock of the outlying grocery stores, they were empty. The food stores at the presidio were all that was available to feed the city. Aid from outside the city was forthcoming immediately.

Communications problems were also quickly solved. Such telephone and telegraph lines as could be used were reserved for official use but a registration system was set up which made it possible to locate nearly everyone in the city. Barrels containing pencils and writing paper were placed near the bread lines, notes were written and deposited in another barrel from which they were collected and distributed throughout the country. By April 21, a regular mail service was in operation.

The fire burned out on Saturday, April 21st. In those 72 hours, four-fifths of the city burned to the ground – 521 blocks containing 28,000 buildings. The much-criticized steel frame buildings withstood the quake and vindicated their proponents. Also standing, untouched by the fire which took its neighbors, was the Mission Dolores. The mission and the house built for the original commandante at the presidio, are the oldest buildings in a city where nothing is more than 207 years old and few things more than 77.

The brand new city hall, built at great expense over a period of many years, collapsed. Rather, half of it collapsed while the rest remained standing. There was a tendency on the part of the populace to attribute this directly to a disparity in the general honesty of the administrations under which portions of the structure had been erected.

Within a week, one cable car line was functioning and a matinee performance was presented at the Orpheum Theater. Stores and restaurants opened for business in private homes, banks built sheds over their vaults and opened their doors to customers. Railroad tracks were built

to carry rubble away. Within three months, 6,000 buildings were under construction. By 1909 a new city had been built.

San Francisco took as her symbol the phoenix rising from the ashes. Ashes are difficult to depict, however, and incorporated into the city's crest is a phoenix shown rising from flames which does tend to look, just a little, like a bird attempting to rectify a regrettable mistake in his choice of a perch.

Early San Francisco was isolated from the rest of the continent. People said it was easier to have a shirt laundered in China than to send a letter to Missouri. It was 25 uncomfortable days by stagecoach to St. Joseph. The uncertain trip by water took 75 days. A young engineer named Theodore Judah wanted to build a railroad. A railway line had been built between San Francisco and San Jose at the south end of the peninsula and had taken three years to complete. The locomotive had to be brought by boat as did everything else at that time. Judah had a great deal of difficulty finding anyone willing to invest in his plan to lay track over the mountains to connect with the line being built from the east. Finally, the times were right. Storekeepers realized that the railroad would enable them to sell their goods to the miners in the silver country. Civil war was coming and President Lincoln needed the gold and silver from California and Nevada to maintain the currency. Also, he wanted a link between east and west in the event of an attack from outside the country. At that time, most of the west was unsettled. Settled being defined as more than two people per square mile. The Central Pacific Railroad Company was formed in 1861. Its members included Leland Stanford, Collis Huntington, Charles Crocker and Mark Hopkins, who came to be known afterward as the Big Four. Judah had his plans ready. He had crossed back and forth over the mountains 73 times while developing them. He went to Washington and helped draft a Pacific Railroad Bill which President Lincoln signed in 1862. The company didn't have much money but it didn't need much. Not of its own. Any community which refused to pay for a portion of the road would be passed by and consigned to oblivion. Besides, the government subsidized the building of the railroad with land, equipment and money. People in Washington were not familiar with the terrain and had no way of knowing that they were often paying for levelling hills that never existed. Judah allowed himself to be bought out after the state geologist allowed his faith in the project to move the mountains twenty miles into the valley. Judah did take an option to buy out the others, however, intending to sell to the Vanderbilts for their collection. He died before he could do this. The Big Four also saved money by importing Chinese laborers and paying them poorly. When the railroad was completed, thousands of the Chinese laborers went to San Francisco where they were resented by a population nearly half of which was unemployed.

The tracks crossed the mountains at Donner Pass where so many members of the Donner Party had died trying to cross only 20 years before. The two sections of the railroad were joined at Promontory, Utah in 1869. The transcontinental railroad ended at Sacramento. The Big Four acquired the two lines connecting Sacramento and Oakland and then branched out into the ferry boat business to bring passengers into San Francisco. What author Frank Norris was to call "The Octopus" had begun: an economic and political stranglehold on San Francisco for many years to come.

The company proceeded to default on government obligations, set rates, restrain competition and buy political officials. For nearly twenty years, all aspects of city politics were controlled by the railroad men through "Blind Boss" Christopher Buckley. In 1881, public outcry resulted in the creation of a commission to oversee the activities of the railroad. Stanford and Huntington named two of the three members. Each of the Big Four left estates valued at forty to fifty million dollars.

The history of finance in San Francisco was as chaotic as everything else. Prior to the discovery of gold there wasn't much money to speak of. Storekeepers acted as bankers. Suddenly there was an influx of people from many different countries; mining gold, buying and selling, providing services and engaging in every imaginable commercial activity. There was no standard currency. Coins from every country were accepted at whatever value could be agreed on. For a while, an 8-inch gold wire was used as the equivalent of one dollar. This was broken up and used in "bits" which is, no doubt, why a quarter of a dollar is still known as "two bits." As many as fourteen companies were issuing their own

coinage on the spot and the value of identical denominations differed according to the source. The price of gold fluctuated wildly. No standard was achieved until a government mint was located in San Francisco in 1854. The next year the price of gold was fixed at $16.00 per ounce.

The first commercial bank was established in 1849 and was followed by more than forty more over the next few years. In 1855 more than twenty of them closed their doors overnight after one of the several financial panics attendant upon an economy based largely on speculation in land and mines.

About the time the goldfields started producing less and less gold, silver was found in Nevada and the whole thing started up again. Silver mines, for a short time, were paying stockholders dividends totalling twenty-five million dollars each month. Everyone wanted to invest in silver and no one wanted to invest in anything else. A stock trading board was established in 1861. Brokers, all with instructions to buy into silver, had to be accompanied by policemen. Men and women sold stock shares on street corners. Rumors of the "big bonanza" or of a mine about to play out were enough to cause a sharp swing in the boom and bust cycle. The rumors often came from a ring of silver speculators who made fortunes manipulating the price of shares. This unstable system crashed for good in 1875 when the Bank of California closed its doors causing all trading on the stock exchange to be suspended.

The Bank of California was started by William Ralston, one of San Francisco's success stories. He had worked on a Mississippi steamboat before coming to California in 1850. He became a partner in a banking house and later formed the Bank of California. He was free with his money. He built and stood the losses of a theater. He built one hotel and decided it wasn't grand enough. He set to work planning the Palace Hotel. He bought a ranch to obtain planks for the hotel and then decided to import them from South America. He acquired a manufacturing company to provide the furniture. On two and a half acres he erected a seven-story, eight-hundred room hotel with a marble-paved courtyard which became a center for San Francisco society until it burned in 1906. Ralston didn't live to see the hotel open. Some of the money Ralston was so free with wasn't his own. He had borrowed from the bank for his own use. He had also disposed of gold bullion. An investigation into allegations of over-issued stock revealed that the bank's vaults held only a half of a million dollars instead of the two millions which were supposed to be there. Ralston resigned as president of the bank and went out to take his customary daily swim. His body was found in the bay later that day.

After the Bank of California closed its doors, a clearing house and a banking commission were established despite considerable opposition from those who had become adept at manipulating the ebb and flow of money. Regulation had its effect. Only two banks have failed here since 1920 and one of those was the Bank of Canton which failed during a revolution in China. San Francisco banks did not suffer the fate of so many others in the stock market crash of 1929. Bankers met and set up a fund which guaranteed the solvency of all the city's banks. Two banks, Wells Fargo, which started life as an express company to carry gold to the east, and the Hibernia Savings and Loan, have been doing business uninterruptedly since they were founded in the early days of San Francisco.

The most successful bank was the Bank of America. It was founded by Amadeo Peter Giannini as the Bank of Italy. This bank became successful by soliciting small deposits from people who up until that time had not bothered with banks. Giannini's lack of the same facilities enjoyed by larger banks worked in his favor during the earthquake. He was able to load his assets and records into a wagon and remove them to his home outside of the city before the fire came. The next day he was able to issue a circular letter advising his depositors that their money was available. Giannini also introduced branch banking which enabled him to pay dividends despite the condition of the local economy. In a financial low period in 1907, Giannini advertised for borrowers.

Today the Bank of America is the largest bank in the world and San Francisco is one of the financial capitals of the world. It is the headquarters of the twelfth Federal Reserve District and the home of the Pacific Stock Exchange even though efforts have been made in recent years to have it moved to Los Angeles. The old mint building survived the fire and, while it isn't making any money these days either, it does contain a museum with an interesting collection of early San

Francisciana.

Many fortunes were made as a result of the gold rush but not necessarily by those working the fields. Money came easily to the early miners but it went just as fast. The one rigorously enforced law was that of supply and demand. Sleeping space on tables, benches, floors and planks was rented for eight hours at hotel prices. Food was sold for prices that would make us gasp today. Some things, tacks for instance, were literally worth their weight in gold. Services came high also. Laundry was so poorly done and so expensive that some of the wealthy actually sent theirs to China to be done.

Later, the market became glutted with too much of everything including things that no one could possibly use. Storage space cost more than the value of the goods and expensive items were left on the streets. Sometimes they were thrown into the streets to try to keep them from becoming sinkholes in which animals became mired and often drowned.

John Sutter, in whose mill race the gold was found, got no good of it. His employees left and his mill fell to ruin. His crops were destroyed and his horses and land were stolen. James Marshall, the man who discovered the gold, fared so badly that years later a benefit was held to raise money for him. He was eventually granted a very small government pension. The ones who got rich were the ones who provided goods and services to the miners. There was money to be had; between 1850 and 1853 gold was brought out of the goldfields at the rate of sixty-five million dollars worth per year. A lot of it went to people who had something the miners needed. One such was Levi Strauss who came intending to provide tents and found that sturdy pants were more in demand. He sent back east for more canvas and began manufacturing his "Levi's." Domingo Ghirardelli came to work in the goldfields but found it was more profitable to grubstake miners. He brought six hundred pounds of chocolate from Peru and sold candy, coffee, fruit and pastry. Ghirardelli chocolates are still favorites with candy fanciers. Many of these entrepreneurs emerged from San Francisco's stormy childhood with fortunes ranging from fifteen to forty million dollars.

Naturally, a few of these tended toward the eccentric. Henry Cogswell was a cotton mill worker who became a successful real estate speculator. He was a teetotaller who distributed twenty drinking fountains to the city, having concluded that people drank liquor because there was insufficient water handy for the purpose. All of the fountains carried life-sized busts of Cogswell. Not all of them were placed; all of them were removed, however. San Franciscans don't have to turn to alcohol. There is still the thirty-four foot tall drinking fountain on Market Street which was the gift of Lotta Crabtree. Charlotte Crabtree was a child prodigy who sang, danced, played the banjo and performed as Little Nell. She amassed a fortune of four million dollars and went to live as a recluse in a Boston hotel. When she died she left her money to aid World War I veterans, antivivisectionists and parolled prisoners.

James Lick belonged to that oxymoronic subgroup of eccentrics, the philanthropic misers. He built a mill near San Jose where he housed and fed his workers exceptionally well while he himself lived in a shanty and ate poorly. He built Lick House but lived in one room, wore old clothes, and carried a sack through the streets collecting bones for fertilizer. On the other hand, he built bath houses for the needy and gave generously to orphan asylums and animal shelters. It was Lick who donated the land for the California Academy of Sciences. He was responsible for the conservatory in Golden Gate Park. Also for the park he erected a monument to Francis Scott Key, the author of "The Star-Spangled Banner" which has the distinction of containing what must be the longest, most incomprehensible, run-on sentence in the English language. Lick had planned to build an observatory at the corner of 4th and Market Streets but was persuaded that an elevated piece of ground would be more suitable to the undertaking. The observatory was built on Mt. Hamilton at the southern end of the peninsula and later became part of the University of California. Lick was buried there.

San Francisco's very favorite character was Joseph Norton. Norton made a fortune in grain speculation but he wasn't happy. He wanted to corner the rice market. This proved to be too much for him. When he couldn't meet the contract price for grain he had ordered, he offered instead to marry the daughter of one of his creditors and make her an empress. He proclaimed himself Norton, Emperor of California and Protector of Mexico, by the Grace of God. His imperial garb

consisted of a military uniform, a plumed hat and a sword. When the uniform became shabby he would demand and receive a new one from the city. He abolished political parties because they caused dissension. During the Civil War he was generous with his advice to both Presidents Lincoln and Davis as well as to their respective generals. He was equally generous with his non-existent wealth and presented the city with a "check" for 3.5 million dollars to build a bridge over the bay by way of Yerba Buena Island. The bridge he envisioned was built over fifty years later at a cost of 77 million.

His two dogs, Lazarus and Bumer, had the run of the city. One died after being kicked by a man who was arrested and fined, the other was run over by a fire engine and received a public funeral. Both dogs were stuffed and presented to the de Young Museum which has evidently misplaced them since they are no longer on display.

Emperor Norton died leaving an estate consisting of one gold piece, a one-franc piece and 93,000 shares of worthless mining stock. An autopsy determined that the cause of death was apoplexy. During the autopsy, an examination of his brain was performed. According to a newspaper report, the examination revealed "... no traces of insanity ... although the marks usually found in the brains of insane persons were present (sic)." Doctors felt that this was not proof of insanity, it happening that those same signs were also commonly found in persons of sane mind.

Fifty years after his death, an Emperor Norton Memorial Association was formed which erected a granite monument over his grave inscribed with his full title.

The very suddenness of San Francisco caused many problems. The Village of Yerba Buena had managed nicely with what civil authority there was vested in the alcalde, the mayor. When the population went from fifty to fifty thousand, there was no established system of law or government to cope with the situation. Women composed only 8 percent of the population, and most of the male population was made up of transients. Miners came in from the goldfields to spend whatever they had in bars and gambling houses of which there were from three hundred to a thousand. An area devoted to drinking, gambling and prostitution grew up around the waterfront. Murders averaged two per night, 4,600 in six years. There were twelve policemen; but there was no jail. John W. Geary became the first alcalde under American jurisdiction in an election ordered by the military. He tried to establish a municipal government but most of the appointed officials were more interested in looting the treasury than in creating order.

Ships' captains were advised to avoid San Francisco and sail on to Honolulu. So many of the crew members who availed themselves of San Francisco's hospitality failed to return that the ships were forced to remain in the harbor. The captains solved this problem themselves by "shanghaiing" sailors: sending out thugs to drug them and carry them aboard where they were kept until the ship sailed.

The activities in the waterfront area were controlled by gangs such as the Hounds and the Sydney Ducks. For a while the area was called Sydney Town for the latter group which was composed of ticket-of-leave prisoners from Australia's penal colony. They were there in direct violation of American law, but American law hadn't gotten around to California yet. The only steps taken toward government in the new territory were the extension of the revenue law over it and the designation of San Francisco as a port of entry.

The city was swept by fire six times between 1849 and 1851. The last and worst of these destroyed 22 city blocks. It may have been the suspicion that the Sydney Ducks had been responsible for at least some of these fires that led to the creation of the first vigilance committee in June of 1851. That same month a man named John Jenkins was hanged for stealing a safe from a store even though he protested that he hadn't taken the safe and that he would prefer to be shot. In August, two more men were hanged after having been taken from the new jail by force. Newspaper editorials lamented these events but their displeasure was directed at the necessity of the proceedings on which they all agreed. Eight men had been hanged by the vigilance committee before it disbanded voluntarily. The gangs had been frightened away by the sudden display of civic responsibility but others soon came to take their places in Murderer's Corner and Battle Row. By the 1860s even the sailors were sufficiently impressed by the viciousness of San Francisco's waterfront to call it the Barbary Coast. A municipal government both able and willing to put an end to the Barbary Coast was not found until

1917.

The problems were not confined entirely to the waterfront. A second vigilance committee was formed after publisher James King of William (Bulletin) was shot by James Casey (Weekly Sunday Times) in 1856. Things were not easy for pioneer newspapermen. One was stabbed, one died in a duel and another killed a state senator in a duel. One who had had some kind things to say about states' rights was attacked by a mob after President Lincoln was shot. The Chronicle's Charles Crocker objected to the candidacy for mayor of one Isaac Kalloch. The paper opposed Kalloch in articles liberally sprinkled with such words as "hypocrite," "criminal," "charlatan," "imposter," "swindler" and "debauchee" coupled with adjectives which could only be called derogatory. When this didn't work, Crocker shot and wounded Kalloch. Kalloch survived and was elected. Crocker was later shot by Kalloch's son, who was acquitted on a plea of self-defense.

The desire to put a crimp in someone's political aspirations was thought to be the motivating force behind the duel in which State Senator David Broderick was killed by Judge Daniel Terry. There appeared to be no personal reason for the duel and informed opinion maintained that an opposing party sent Terry to pick a fight with Broderick. Terry was chosen because he was a good shot and because he was about to finish his term under a cloud and wasn't of any further use to the party anyway. Terry was later shot by the bodyguard of another justice whom he attacked in a hotel dining room.

While the absence of government was most visible in San Francisco, it applied to the rest of California as well. General Vallejo, who favored union with the United States in spite of the bear flag incident, organized a constitutional convention to draft a constitution and apply for statehood. California was admitted as a state in 1850. All the towns vied for the privilege of being the state capital except for San Francisco whose citizens may have felt that this was a little more government than they wanted on their doorsteps. The legislature first convened at San Jose but was dissatisfied with the unfinished building in which it was accommodated. General Vallejo offered to build them a capital building in Vallejo but the legislature stayed only a few months. The capital was then permanently fixed at Sacramento.

Immediately, the courts became clogged with cases involving land disputes. Land grants had been the Mexican Governors' favorite method of buying loyalty, repaying loyalty and doing favors generally. Land in California was disposed of liberally. In the area around Monterey millions of acres were controlled by 800 families. In many cases, the more formal aspects of land exchanges, such as written documentation, were neglected. A growing population challenged the grants and the large ranchos were broken up when they were not honored. General Vallejo's claim was upheld but there was no means of enforcing the decision against the squatters on his land. He was left "destitute" with only a few hundred acres.

The cases dragged on for years. Golden Gate Park was eventually built on land to which San Francisco did not get clear title until the mid-1860s.

Eventually the land question was sorted out by one method or another and San Francisco went about the business of becoming a metropolis. The first thing that needed to be done was to diminish California's isolation from the east coast. Crowds gathered in 1860 to cheer the first Pony Express rider on his way. Businessmen were happy to pay five dollars to send a letter that would cross two thousand miles of wilderness in nine days rather than a month. Less than two years later the Pony Express was no longer needed. Some of these businessmen had telegraph wires in their homes.

Soon wealth brought leisure and leisure brought an interest in "society." There was no society to break into, no established traditional order with rigid customs and laws such as existed in the east. Wealthy San Franciscans were able to create their own fashions. Fun was fashionable. So was spending money on fine houses, the showier the better. Horse racing was more than a popular pastime. Attached to the fine houses were stables lavishly constructed with inlaid woods and expensive fixtures. One stable was as large as the house and another was provided with a chandelier. Time was spent visiting, giving parties, going to the theater and the opera, driving in carriages and chartering boats for excursions on the bay. Weekdays were spent on the cocktail circuit. In 1895 there was a population of three hundred

thousand and one saloon for every ninety-six people. They served enormous free lunches in the fashionable places along Sutter, Market and Powell Streets. To say that a man had barroom manners was high praise. Formal attire was worn on the plank sidewalks and in homes lighted with candles or oil lamps. Only the large hotels had gaslight. Society began to take itself very seriously. Private clubs were formed by the elite. One of these was the Pacific Club which occupied quarters once belonging to a gambling hall. An old miner who blundered in was unimpressed on being informed of the change, observing that the clientele hadn't changed at all. New York had its 400 and San Francisco had its 45. These were the champagne days devoted to pleasure, entertainment and gossip which caused Frank Norris to designate San Francisco "the city where nobody thinks."

There were other aspects, of course. The Barbary Coast still flourished with its own kind of entertainment. The more violent activities had abated but drinking, gambling and prostitution were still its main pursuits. None of these things was illegal, however, and no one saw any reason to object to it. On the contrary, so much of the money generated there found its way into influential pockets that, after the earthquake, the section was rebuilt and continued to flourish for another ten years.

Backing up against the Barbary Coast was Chinatown which was, in many ways, just as bad.

The first Chinese to come to California, two men and one woman, arrived aboard the brig Eagle in 1848. The next decade brought twenty-five thousand more either drawn by gold or driven by political upheaval at home. Later, thousands more were brought in to provide the labor for building the railroad for which they were paid sixty-five cents per day. When the railroad was finished, many of the Chinese workers made their way to San Francisco where they were not welcomed by the large numbers of unemployed. There were many small unions whose activity levels rose and fell in response to conditions in the particular field of each one. They united on two issues: the eight-hour day and the resentment of the cheap labor pool provided by the Chinese. The unions regarded these most exploited of workers as enemies of labor and allies of the rich who employed them. Dennis Kearney organized an army of unemployed workers and threatened to burn the city if the Chinese were not driven out. Kearney is said to have been bought off at the price of a new dray but agitation against the Chinese continued and finally resulted in the Chinese Exclusion Act of 1882 which prevented any further immigration from China. The inability of men to send to China for wives resulted in what amounted to a slave traffic in Chinese girls. The Act also excluded many of the Chinese already here from engaging in their customary occupations making it even more difficult to earn a living than it had been before. Criminal activity thrived. The Chinese were not welcomed outside of Chinatown. Nearly thirty thousand people were confined in an area measured in blocks. Chinatown was a slum; poor, overcrowded, and violent.

In the midst of the notorious violence and crime of Chinatown, ordinary residents carried on their daily lives in as traditional a manner as possible. They worked, worshipped, raised families and survived. Nearly all had come from the same province and spoke the same language. Civil affairs were handled within the community under the direction of the Six Companies. After Chinatown burned down in 1906 there was some talk of relocating it elsewhere. Much of the talk came from real estate speculators who realized that the area occupied by the Chinese had become a very desirable location. They weren't given the chance. Chinatown was rebuilt quickly with money from within the community.

San Francisco's Chinese population is not the largest outside of China but it is the largest in proportion to the rest of the population. It is still one of the most congested neighborhoods in a densly-populated city. Every year thousands of newcomers arrive to try to make their way in an unfamiliar place. They will join the others who live and work in the crowded section regarded by many as a tourist attraction. Many of the newcomers are from other districts of China and speak dialects other than Cantonese. They may face problems as difficult as those faced by the earlier immigrants trying to preserve their culture amidst an alien one.

The Chinese have moved out of Chinatown in more than a physical sense. They take an active part in civic affairs and contribute to all aspects of life in the city. They have even created a museum which offers a glimpse of the history of their struggle to maintain themselves here, a struggle too admirable to be neglected.

When San Franciscans built their permanent buildings, they built them to look exactly like whatever they had left behind. Houses appeared that could have been set down anywhere in New England without looking out of place. The British and the French constructed homes conforming to their country's interpretation of the Roman style. Nearly all the houses were made of wood.

Wood was plentiful, while other materials were not available at first and weren't required by the temperate climate. Besides, the earth had a tendency to shake here and it was thought that wood would prove more flexible in the face of the demands placed on it by terra-less-than-firma. Some churches and most public buildings favored the heavy masonry style traditional in Europe but there were no facilities for local quarrying. Granite for these buildings was brought from China which was easier than bringing it overland from the east. It wasn't all that easy. Of the first 20,000 buildings no more than six were made of stone. Bricks were used instead and were being produced on a large scale by 1849. Wood was still favored and the technique of balloon-frame construction enabled houses to be put up rapidly. This method used mass-produced nails instead of mortises and tenons and substituted 2″ x 4″ studs in place of the heavier frames used previously. The name was bestowed by critics convinced that the dwellings would sail away in the first high wind.

Fire was, and is yet, a major concern. In 1853 a law went into effect prohibiting any structure not made of stone or brick from being erected in the financial district. Where sufficient money was available, owners favored granite foundations, 4-foot thick brick walls and heavy iron doors and shutters. One of the first establishments to be so well protected was a popular gambling house on Portsmouth Square. When the invention of the cable car made the hills accessible, the wealthy built houses on them which combined regional tradition and materials with a penchant for truly vulgar ostentation and conspicuous consumption. They built wooden Gothic monstrosities and painted them in colors which were intended to make them resemble stone.

The U.S. government favored a Greek revival style for its buildings such as the customs house and post office, which was designed in Boston, and the mint. Hotels chose either Greek revival or English Roman while the churches evidenced a belief that God is best served in Gothic.

The only structures which could be considered as belonging particularly to San Francisco were the Victorians. Most of these were put up in a building spree in the 1880s and 1890s. There was no architectural innovation involved in the design of these houses. Most of them were simply plain wood frame houses with flat roofs built shoulder to shoulder up and down the hills. They were row houses, without distinction, functional. Except for the facade. It was found that the plentiful redwood was easily turned and lent itself to decorative scrollwork. In a reaction against the merely functional, people took to decorating the fronts of their houses as elaborately as they could. Anyone could do it. Catalogues of machine-made ornamentation were offered to the homebuilder who could express his own personality by mixing and matching whatever appealed to him. Quoins and columns, flowers and filigree, motifs copied from ornamental stonework, all these graced the exteriors of the homes in an attempt to escape the confinement of a narrow city lot. The style was sometimes described as a mixture of Queen Anne and Eastlake. Eastlake himself, while no doubt grateful for the honor, dissociated himself from the Victorians in a statement containing such words as "burlesque" and "bizarre". On the other hand, no one seemed to be quite sure what he meant by Queen Anne style. The only description of an architecture style that I ever came close to understanding was one taken from an 1877 issue of American Architect which described Queen Anne style as "any eccentricity in general design that one can suppose would have occurred to designers 150 or 200 years ago." There. Now you know what the Victorians look like. They were generally referred to as "carpenter Gothic."

One of the features shared by all the Victorians and nearly every other house built at the same time was the bay window. 95 percent of the homes sported them. The Palace Hotel had 400 bay windows. They were needed to admit the maximum amount of air and light to houses built close against each other. Those with more money to spend opted for five-sided bays. More common was the three-sided rectangular bay found on those houses which came to be called "San Francisco stick." These all had split facades with the bay window on one side and a column-supported porch on the other.

Preservation of the historical has become important in most major cities. Perhaps it is even more important in San Francisco where what might now have been of historical interest did not simply give way, while it was still the everyday, to the new but was abruptly removed by a power greater than that of any developer or urban planning commission. A good many of the Victorians, especially in the neighborhood known as the western addition even though subsequent additions from the west has placed it fairly well in the middle of the city, survived the fire in 1906. These are now being restored. When they were first built they received no critical acclaim whatsoever. They were attacked as being too "busy" and for violating whole cartloads of architectural principles. The row houses especially were panned as discouraging. Today they are finding friends who regard them as an integral part of San Francisco's heritage. Restored, and painted in bright colors, the blues and reds and yellows which their original owners chose for them, they are eye-catching and appealing. They are to San Francisco what the brownstone is to New York City and they belong here.

Another building that survived the earthquake and fire to become a central feature of the city's skyline is the Ferry Building. It was built in the 1890s when it was thought that the best buildings were those modelled after ones existing somewhere else, preferably Europe. In the case of the Ferry Building, the model was Seville's Giralda Tower. For years it was one of the busiest terminals anywhere. Commuters coming to work in San Francisco poured in from communities all over the Bay area. Until 1958 when the ferries connecting San Francisco with the railway terminus in Oakland were discontinued, the Ferry Building was the arrival point for all the people coming to the city at the end of the transcontinental railroad. It is still a center of activity as it now houses the World Trade Center where its interests lie to the west rather than to the east. While many people may recognize another San Francisco building as the setting for one of those movies regaling its audiences with the antics of people trapped by fire in a highrise, the Ferry Building also had its moment in the annals of film entertainment.

Willis Polk designed so many post-earthquake buildings that he became known as the man who rebuilt San Francisco. He and his designs were so popular that by the time it was discovered that he didn't have an architect's license, nobody cared. One of his contributions was the Hobart building, the first to be architecturally finished on all four sides rather than on the street side only. Another of his buildings was the Hallidie building, designed on commission from the University of California which allowed him a free hand. His design introduced a feature that was a preview of the modern skyscraper, a facade of glass. Architects and builders knew that steel-frame construction did not require massive outer walls; they also knew that tradition did, even if it meant adding a false front to a building. Polk's one sop to tradition was the inclusion of ornamental ironwork in the facade into which he managed to incorporate the fire escapes. The combination is distinctive even today. In 1918 derisible was more the word for it. It was received with so many hoots and gibes that nothing like it was tried again for many years afterward.

The idea of a civic center complex was conceived in 1904 but was not acted upon because too many buildings would have had to have been bought up for the purpose. In 1906 this obstacle was removed. Arthur Brown, Jr., a graduate of the Ecole des Beaux Arts of Paris, designed the new city hall which was completed in 1915. A splendid, colonnaded classic affair, it was the city's pride. One didn't have to inquire to be told that the mammoth dome was higher than the capitol dome in Washington, D.C.

Efforts were made right after the fire to build a municipal opera house but the necessary money was not forthcoming. In 1920 someone had the idea of building an opera house as a war memorial. Funds were solicited and $2,150,000 was raised in the first twenty days. The opera house was also designed by Arthur Brown, Jr. who was not about to depart from the classical formula which had been so successful. He did, however, choose to incorporate some features introduced by Wagner at the Bayreuth opera house. Wagner had proceeded on the premise that the performance was more important than the audience. This point of view required that all seats face the stage, that the stage be enlarged and that musicians should be heard and not seen. The first performance at the War Memorial Opera House was given on Oct. 15, 1932 to a full house. The opera house was also the site of the United Nations Charter conference in 1945.

The 1920s were years of affluence and a bustle of building was in progress. Early height restrictions for certain classes of buildings had been removed in 1907. It was an era of skyscrapers, if moderate-sized structures trying to pass themselves off as something else – houses of worship, perhaps – could be considered skyscrapers. Traditional Roman and Gothic massive was still the going thing, especially if it was a copy of something else. (The original plan for the Golden Gate bridge called for an approach resembling the Arc de Triomphe.) Many of the new buildings were the work of George Kelham, a popular commercial architect who had come from New York to oversee the reconstruction of the Palace Hotel. His contributions include the Federal Reserve Bank and the city's first real skyscraper, a 22-story building put up by Standard Oil.

There were some departures from the tried and tired. One of these was the Telephone Building designed by Timothy Pfleuger. Pfleuger's plans were inspired by an unused design submitted to a Chicago competition. Chicago got another gothic building and San Francisco got something different; something built on vertical lines, unabashedly a skyscraper, with none of the embellishments used by more conventional structures to disguise the fact. Another of Pfleuger's buildings is known simply by its address, 450 Sutter. Here he approached Polk's glass wall design and combined it with an old favorite, bayed windows. He also added an underground parking garage and a rooftop solarium. Many people would have been a great deal happier today if more designers had thought to incorporate the former in their plans.

Pfleuger was also responsible for the Pacific Stock Exchange building for which Diego Rivera was called in to paint murals. I do not know whether there was any of the fuss which occurred in New York when Rivera used a head of Lenin to adorn a Rockefeller wall. A stock exchange seems to be as good a place for a proletarian fresco as Rockefeller Center.

This spurt of building ended in the 30s with the coming of depression and war and was not resumed again until the 50s.

The building boom of the fifties took San Francisco to the limit of its lateral expansion. On the north and east, the city had helped itself to huge areas belonging to the bay. Now it had come up against the Pacific and no compromise was possible. There was nowhere to go but up. Here entered the dread spectre of "Manhattanization."

The battle between the upbuilders and their opponents is a grim one. The builders have on their side that overriding force in all human affairs, economic reality. Cities can't just stop any more than any other living thing can. Growth is unavoidable and parks are not good investments. Limited space means limited options. Industry moved out of the city to places where there was room to sprawl. San Francisco's main industries are tourism, services and finance. People pour into the city every morning and pour out again at night leaving behind them no tangible commodity. With the exception of sour dough bread and steam beer – there are always some necessities. The port declined when San Francisco was slower than Oakland to appreciate the possibilities of containerized freight. At the end of the fifties, it was considered a conservative estimate that the population of San Francisco would double in the next three decades. In 1950 the population was 775,000. In 1980 it was 678,974. Who left, and why? A better question is "Where were they when they were here?" There is no affordable housing now. What is built, and how much of it, will determine who can live here. Families find it extremely difficult to find housing they can afford. The logic of the thing is inexorable. More and more people will be forced out and San Francisco will lose the diversity which has been such an important factor in its development.

What is built will also determine the character of the city. The most successful methods have been to combine the old and the new. The favorite shopping areas are not suburban malls but places like Ghirardelli Square, a complex of modern shops located in refurbished factory buildings. Or the Cannery which was a fruit packing plant in pre-earthquake days. On Union Street, wares are displayed in restored Victorians. The Embarcadero Center complex is new but consideration was given to open air spaces with statues and fountains. If there must be highrises, at least let them be like the Hyatt Regency Hotel which has a lobby people come especially to see. When was the last time you went out to tour a hotel lobby?

There will always be people who will come to the defense of anything which they feel contributes to the quality of a city they care about. The same people who stopped the construction on the Embarcadero Freeway before it was completed and who now want the completed portion removed will put up a fight to preserve what they have. They do not want to live in canyons. They do not want their homes to look like places to which people are committed involuntarily. They know that if the light and air and sense of spaciousness lent by the hills are to be negated, if San Francisco is not to be a city of vistas, then there is no point to it.

Driving in San Francisco, once you have mastered the art of starting and stopping on hills, is not difficult. But parking is impossible. It doesn't matter. San Francisco is for walking in and the best way to see it is on foot. By geography, history and culture, the city is divided into neighborhoods or districts. It is less a unified metropolis than a collection of communities. The populations and the boundaries of these communities tend to shift a lot, however.

The financial district is built on landfill that was once Yerba Buena Cove. The rotten hulls of ships deserted by their crews lie underneath, grounded forever. Its principal street is Montgomery St., "the Wall Street of the West." It was named after John Montgomery who first raised the American Flag over Portsmouth Square. He probably wouldn't have appreciated this honor at first. The street was a mire even after attempts were made to solidify it by throwing in bales of material, tobacco, old stove parts and anything else that might be available.

Even so, it was not so bad as Kearny Street which was pronounced to be "not even Jackassable" by an unknown early poet. It was the first to be paved when the city finally got around to such things in 1854.

At first glance, everything appears to be a bank but if you look around you can find a few other things. If you look up you can see the Transamerica Pyramid. If you like, you can go to the observation deck on the twenty-seventh floor which is open to the public, but there are better places from which to look out over San Francisco. The pyramid was built on the site of one of the city's first buildings, the Montgomery Block. This was a four-story brick building erected in 1853. Because it was thought to be fire-proof, Adolph Sutro's two million dollar book collection was housed there. Dr. Sun Yat-Sen wrote the Chinese Constitution in one of the building's offices. Mark Twain, Bret Harte, Robert Louis Stevenson, Rudyard Kipling and Jack London either worked in the offices or drank in the bar. During the 1906 fire, dynamite charges were planted but not detonated because of pleas to save the books. Another part of the collection stored in a house on Battery Street was lost.

Telegraph Hill was so named because it was the site of a semaphore station linked by telegraph to Point Lobos on the western shore. News of arriving ships was telegraphed to the station and signalled to the townspeople who would rush to meet the ships. Today, it is the site of Coit Tower.

Lillie Hitchcock Coit was rescued from a fire as a child and developed a fascination with firefighting. She went far beyond the usual manifestations of fire buffery. She had a costume, including a helmet, in which she accompanied her favorite, volunteer fire company 5, on every call. She wore a gold badge, which was given to her by the company, all the time, even in evening dress. She would leave a party, a dance or, in one case, a wedding in which she was a bridesmaid, to attend a fire. She was made an honorary member of the brigade, rode with them in parades and attended their banquets. She had the number 5 embroidered on all her clothes. When she died, she left money for a monument to firefighters which was erected in Washington Square. She also left a large bequest for the purpose of beautifying San Francisco. The money was used to build a fluted column on the top of Telegraph Hill. It stands five hundred and forty feet high and is topped with a glass-enclosed observation deck which commands a fine view of both the city and the bay. The tower was completed in the 1930s and received mixed reviews. Not everyone agreed that the "damn silo" had any appreciable effect on the beauty of the city. A few years later, twenty-five artists were commissioned to decorate the walls with murals depicting scenes of life in California.

The cottages clinging to the steep slopes of Telegraph Hill have always been desirable residences. This neighborhood was the first to have a community association. The Telegraph

Hill Neighborhood Association was formed in 1890.

Southeast of Telegraph Hill is Russian Hill. It may have been named for a cemetery for Russian sailors located nearby but we're guessing. Other suggestions will be entertained. This hill also was originally dotted with small cottages much favored by artists and writers but, because there was more level ground here than on Telegraph Hill, larger, more expensive dwellings were built. These, in turn, are being replaced by apartment buildings. A few of the houses at the top of the hill escaped the fire in 1906. The oldest one dates back to 1853.

Just south of Russian Hill is a hill which was called Fern Hill in the gold rush days but which became Nob (read snob or nabob) Hill after San Francisco's wealthy, including the Big Four, who chose to display their wealth by building ostentatious houses on it. These were completely destroyed by the earthquake and subsequent fire and were not greatly missed. The Pacific Union Club was built over the remains of one. The Mark Hopkins Hotel stands on the site of his old residence and the site of the Crocker mansion is now occupied by Grace Cathedral.

The burned-out nobs moved west to Pacific Heights where they rebuilt with either vastly improved taste or more sensitivity to the opinions of their fellow citizens. The old Gothic monstrosities were replaced by Georgian, Classic Corinthian, and Tudor residences according to individual preference. Some of these old mansions have become schools or clubs and apartment buildings have made encroachments here also. There may be more resistance to them here since they have not infiltrated to the same extent as they have elsewhere. The view of the bay and the bridge are well worth protecting.

Union Street is a six-block stretch of fashionable shops and restaurants, stylish, expensive and not at all the sort of place early residents would ever expect to find next to Washerwoman's Lagoon in a valley once inhabited almost exclusively by cows. The cows were banished when the residents of Pacific Heights became particular about their neighbors. The lagoon is gone as well. This district, still known as Cow Hollow, is another that once fronted a small cove. In 1915 San Francisco hosted a Panama-Pacific

Exposition to celebrate the opening of the Panama Canal. One hundred eighty-four acres were reclaimed from the bay to serve as an exposition ground. One of the buildings built for this exposition was the Palace of Fine Arts. Designed to resemble a Roman ruin, it was one of ten such buildings built around a courtyard. This particular one was so popular that when the other buildings were torn down, the Palace of Fine Arts was left standing. It had not been built for permanence, however, and would have had to have been removed but for Walter Johnson's public-spirited donation of 2 million dollars in 1959. He said that if the city liked the place as much as he did, between the two of them it could be rebuilt as a permanent fixture. The city agreed. The Palace overlooks a small pond and attracts many visitors including a number of ducks, which the other visitors feed, and sea gulls who steal the food from the ducks. This building is a favorite for two reasons. One reason is that so much money was spent to preserve a structure having no practical value whatsoever simply because it was appealing. The second is the fact that it houses the Exploratorium. This is a science hall. But don't tell the children; they think it's a playground. It features exhibits demonstrating scientific principles and placards and guides are available to provide you with just as much explanation as you feel capable of taking in. The attitude of the proprietors is "touch everything; you can't hurt it and it can't hurt you." Everything may be handled, tried, used and enjoyed even by the youngest and the clumsiest.

The cove which was filled in to create the exposition ground is now the Marina District. There was some discussion of what to do with the land after the exposition ended. A compromise was reached. The waterfront area was used in part for a yacht harbor. The rest became a park; the Marina Green. The Green is a haven for strollers, sun worshippers and kite flyers.

The remainder of the land was zoned for residences but it was several years before the offer was taken up. Perhaps people were leery of building their homes on landfill. When homes were built, a Spanish theme was followed with tiled roofs, ironwork and arches on the stucco houses. The street names, such as Cervantes, Avila and Toledo, carry on the theme.

If you go north over Russian Hill you will come to Fisherman's Wharf. This is a very good place to go if you want to see a lot of people. The wharf doesn't pretend to be much other than a tourist spot. There is still commercial fishing activity but the fishermen are up and away before the rest of us good folk. Restaurants sprang up where fishermen used to sell their catch from the boats. The restaurants are good so it's worth a trip even if you don't want to charter a boat for a tour of the bay or take a helicopter ride. Alternatively, you can visit the attractive shops on Pier 39.

Don't miss the Maritime Museum. You can't miss it. It's in that concrete building in the shape of a ship. If you're not much interested in nautical artifacts but like boats, you're in luck. Part of the museum floats. Take a tour of the lumber schooner, the C.A. Thayer, the steam schooner, Wapama, the Eureka and the Alma. The prize is the Balclutha, a square-rigger which sailed around the Horn seventeen times in the late 1800s. The Balclutha was only a shell when the museum acquired it but it was completely restored through the efforts of several different labor unions whose members donated their time to the project.

Portsmouth Square is the heart of what used to Yerba Buena Village before someone decided that the city should have the same name as the bay. It was in this square that Montgomery first raised the American flag and here also that Sam Brannan announced the discovery of gold. The first house was built nearby in 1835 on Grant Street. Nearby also was the customs house, built by the Mexican Government in 1844. It was from this four-room adobe house that John Jenkins was hanged by the first vigilance committee at two o'clock in the morning following a hasty trial. The face of Portsmouth Square has changed. Today it is a garden park lying over an underground parking garage. If you look at Portsmouth Square on the map you will realize just how much of the bay has been filled-in to enlarge San Francisco. Montgomery mounted his guns on Battery Street which isn't near the waterfront either.

Grant Street is now the center but not necessarily the heart of Chinatown. Here is the much-photographed Chinatown Gate, inscribed with a quotation from Dr. Sun Yat-Sen which was donated to San Francisco by the people of Shanghai. Grant Street is colorful and exotic and busy. Tourists throng the curio shops and Chinese who no longer live there come to shop in the food stores.

Despite the occasional reference to the Latin Quarter, North Beach is North Beach. It is at least as heterogeneous as any neighborhood in the city but there is still a distinct Italian flavor. Italian restaurants and cafes, bocce courts and sausage makers can be found throughout the area. You might detect a Bohemian note as well, no doubt a holdover from the days when Jack Kerouac, Allen Ginsberg and Lawrence Ferlinghetti brought the beat generation to North Beach. They attracted a group of followers and hangers-on who brought a good deal of publicity to the neighborhood and made some people very nervous, indeed. By the early 1960s it was felt that the beatnik era would pass without leaving any impression. It was becoming expensive to live in North Beach and many of the hangers-on were moving away into cheaper quarters in an undistinguished area near Haight and Ashbury Streets. North Beach blends into Chinatown and the financial district at Broadway, a neon strip of a pseudo-sleazy sort, more tacky than wicked and not entirely without humor.

The Mission District takes its name from the Mission Dolores as does its principal street, Mission Street. After fire destroyed their homes in the district to the east, the residents moved out into the Mission District. It was once an Irish enclave but has now become, appropriately enough, a Spanish community. Its situation, in a valley protected by surrounding heights from fog and wind, provides the Mission District with the balmiest weather of any place in San Francisco.

Most of San Francisco's oldest structures are to be found in the district called the Western Addition. This is located slightly more east than west but does lie to the west of Van Ness Avenue, the point at which the 1906 fire finally burned out. A large collection of Victorian houses is to be found here. This quiet neighborhood became the business district after the fire but only until the downtown area was rebuilt. It was a Japanese neighborhood until the early 1940s. At that time the Japanese were removed to camps, leaving their homes to house workers who flocked to San Francisco to work in the shipyards. To accommodate as many people as possible, the houses were divided into small apartments by owners who then went to live elsewhere, neglecting to keep up the buildings. Some of them had been covered with stucco or asbestos shingles following the fire. After the war, some of the Japanese moved back to the neighborhood only to be dispossessed by plans for a Japanese Cultural and Trade Center.

The Victorians are being restored one by one. Neighborhood associations such as the Western Addition Project Area Committee are working to find methods by which the houses can be restored and owned by residents of the neighborhood rather than by urban renewers.

The Richmond District lies along the ocean with Golden Gate Park to the south and the Golden Gate Bridge to the north. The name is simply one of many the residents could have chosen that was more elegant than The Great Sandy Waste, the name by which everything west of Twin Peaks was known. It is a middle-class residential district which lacks the topographical and architectural diversity of the older parts of San Francisco. There are people who say that the Richmond, together with the Sunset District, its neighbor on the other side of the park, are not really part of the city at all. The sayers have a point although a debatable one depending on who gets to define the terms. Admittedly, "the avenues" as they are called are not, yet, quintessentially San Francisco. Quintessential or not, the Richmond district is an attractive place to live. The nearness to the ocean and the park make it desirable. Also here is Lincoln Park in which is located the California Palace of the Legion of Honor. The building, modelled after the Palais de la Legion d'Honneur in Paris, was erected as a memorial to the California veterans of World War 1. Among the many exhibits are forty Rodin bronzes and marbles, including a cast of the Thinker which stands in the courtyard, a collection of Egyptian art and numerous pieces of French sculpture. The French Government presented the museum with a set of Gobelin tapestries. Many collections came as gifts to the memorial, including one of 17th century Flemish and Dutch paintings. A fund was establised to acquire the works of California artists. The museum offers temporary exhibits in addition to its permanent collection. The Palace also contains a small theater.

If you're not in the mood to meander through the museum, Lincoln Park also has a golf course. If you just want to walk, take a stroll through the grounds. The park land was once a burial ground for both unknown sailors and Chinese who were interred here until their bones could be returned to China. Somewhere in the shrubbery you will come across a bronze obelisk perpetrated by Henry Cogswell of drinking fountain fame. I am not exactly sure just what it is that Cogswell intended to commemorate here. The best place to walk is along the cliff to Land's End which takes in some of the finest scenery anywhere. Wind and water have taken a heavy toll on the cliffs. Climbing them is emphatically discouraged by air-sea rescue squads and emergency room physicians.

From your vantage point at Land's End you can look down on the Cliff House, Seal Rocks and Ocean Beach. The seals on Seal Rocks are actually Stellar Sea Lions but they look very much like seals especially from a distance and that's good enough for me. The seals are citizens of San Francisco but there are fewer of them all the time as they retreat to the Farallones or to their breeding grounds further down the coast. There was once a suspension bridge built to Seal Rocks which was erected by the same outfit that built the Brooklyn Bridge. The latter is still standing, I believe, but the former fell into the water one day. The people on the bridge at the time were saved from the water and the seals were saved from the people so there is nothing to be regretted.

There has been a Cliff House of one sort or another since 1863 when the original was built. It was once a fashionable place to take refreshment after a carriage drive along the Point Lobos Toll Road, now Geary Street. Later, a street car would take people there for 50 cents. That may have been when it became popular rather than fashionable and degenerated into a shabby beer parlor. The original building was damaged in 1887 when a schooner carrying eighty thousand pounds of dynamite was wrecked on the shore below. It finally succumbed to fire in 1894. The second Cliff House, built by Adolph Sutro in 1896 was a rather grand affair, a gingerbread castle with witch-hat turrets at each corner. This structure survived the events of 1906 only to burn down the following year. The seals were so upset that they abandoned their rock for two years. Sutro rebuilt on the site but less extravagantly. An attempt to operate on a teetotal basis during Prohibition was unsuccessful and the Cliff House closed for the duration. The present building was put up in the fifties and has all the excitement generally associated with that decade. You can get a drink there, however. You can also browse through the bookstore which specializes in San Francisco lore, observe the seals through coin-operated binocular machines, visit

the Musee Mechanique, a collection of old mechanical toys and games, or visit the camera obscura. The Cliff House is also a good place from which to observe the complex actions of the waves off Ocean Beach.

Mountain Lake Park is also in the Richmond District. It was by this lake that the expedition led by Juan Batista de Anza camped while selecting the sites for the Presidio and the mission. It was a member of his party who wrote in his diary that there wasn't a tree in sight. An historical marker is located in a grove of trees on the shore of the lake.

It was to the Richmond District that the Chinese came when they began moving out of Chinatown.

The Sunset District was, for the most part, built all at once by one developer, Henry Doelger. He discovered that the only way to defeat the drifting sand was to build wholesale. He erected block after block of white row houses which caused people to refer to the results as "the white cliffs of Doelger." Although the Sunset District was the last area of the city to be developed, one man built his house in the great sand waste in 1840. George Greene brought material all the way from Maine to build his house next to Laguna Puerca which is Spanish for sow lake. The lake is called Pine Lake. During the land grant litigations, Greene built a fort and defended his property until he could get his title confirmed. His son planted the land with eucalyptus trees. Thirty-three acres of this land were donated to the city by Mrs. Sigmund Stern as a memorial to her husband. The land was to be used for cultural and educational activities. Concerts in Stern Grove are very popular.

Lake Merced was originally an inlet from the ocean until drifting sand formed a spit creating the five-acre lake. Eventually, streams replaced the salt water with fresh water and the lake was dammed and used as a reservoir. No longer needed as a reservoir, the lake has been stocked with trout. Nearby is the spot where Senator David Broderick was killed by Judge Daniel Terry.

During the course of your rambles through San Francisco, you may note the absence of cemeteries. There used to be cemeteries here, of course. There were graveyards at Laurel Hill and Lone Mountain as well as other smaller ones. In 1901 a city ordinance prohibited burial within the city limits. Later, the city went further and ordered disinterment and removal from all cemeteries of more than five acres. Today there is only the military cemetery at the Presidio, a portion of the cemetery attached to the Mission Dolores and the Odd Fellows Columbarium. Ex-San Franciscans are buried south of the city in the town of Colma where they constitute the majority of the population.

You will find parks, however. John McClaren may have gotten his wish of having a park within walking distance of every home in San Francisco. Looking at a map of the city, it is heartening to note the numerous splotches of green which represent them. Also look for fountains. In Justin Herman Plaza you will find the Vaillancourt Fountain, hailed by many as the world's ugliest. Keep an eye out for the animal sculptures of Beniamino Bufano which appear here and there. Bufano once said that the only critics he cared about were children. San Franciscans are all for him.

Contrary to what you may have heard, the conservation "fad" is not over. Concern with preserving wilderness areas began quite some time ago in northern California. The Sierra Club was founded in 1892. Four hundred acres of redwood forest known as Muir Woods were declared a national monument in 1908. In 1912 the Mt. Tamalpais Conservation Club was formed.

California has the military to thank for much of its good fortune. Back in the 1850s, the army was already acquiring coastal land for defense purposes. This stepped up quickly during the Civil War. Apparently, the Army was expecting an attack by the British who were believed to be sympathetic to the Confederate cause. The Army prepared for the attack. Between 1860 and 1863, Angel Island was fortified with guns trained on the entrance to the bay. Fort Point, the fort, was built at Fort Point, the point and federal troops moved in in 1861. It was officially called Fort Winfield Scott but it kept getting confused with Fort Scott so it was always called Fort Point. It was the last brick fort built in the United States and the only one built in the west. As was the case with its Spanish predecessor, Fort Point never fired a shot in anger. The British didn't come; nobody came. Still, the Army continued to acquire coastal lands until more sophisticated methods of defense were devised and the land was no longer

required for that purpose. The Army kept the land from being developed for any other purpose so miles and miles of coastline was available for the creation of a National Seashore. In 1972 the Golden Gate National Recreation Area was created. It now controls over one hundred and twenty thousand acres of parklands and there is pressure to add more. Another fifty-two thousand acres are under the control of the East Bay Regional Park District.

The headquarters of the GGNRA are at Fort Mason, another thing to thank the Army for. They built the huge transport docks which have come to be so useful. No one could decide what to do with them so they are available for all sorts of cultural and recreational events. The public library holds its annual book sale there. Christmas trees can be purchased at the appropriate season. At any given time, there is likely to be a crafts fair, a workshop, a play, an exhibition or some other event going on at Fort Mason. The Oceanic Society has quarters there as does Greenpeace.

Several conservation groups have their headquarters in San Francisco. These report an increase in memberships recently. This increase is attributed to spreading alarm at the activities of the present directors of the Environmental Protection Agency who appear to have the conservation instincts of an old buffalo hunter.

The Army is also preserving the Presidio for us. Much of it is open to the public but we benefit from all of it. It provides the city with an expanse of undeveloped land larger in area than Golden Gate Park.

San Francisco was never a typical frontier town. The hordes of people who flocked to the goldfields were as varied a lot as ever assembled anywhere. They were drawn not only by the gold but also by the excitement of being in at the beginning of a new place on which they could leave their mark. The stream flowing to San Francisco brought with it educated and cultured people from various countries. These people were sophisticated enough to demand schools, newspapers, theaters, literary magazines, libraries, music and art and they had the money to get them. Adolph Sutro came to San Francisco after making his fortune in Nevada and bought a piece of land which was about one-tenth of the area of the whole city. When he wasn't planting trees or staging scenes from classical plays in his garden of statuary, he collected a library of two hundred fifty thousand books and manuscripts.

The first entertainment given in San Francisco was in 1849. Within a few years, regular productions were offered. The fare of one production company alternated between circuses and Shakespeare. The combination is typical of San Francisco. Both circuses and Shakespeare are appreciated here. The population cannot be divided into concert goers and baseball fans. San Franciscans had opera before they had paved streets. The world's major cities have always looked down on San Francisco as a cultural wasteland. It was never a place chosen by a would-be concert pianist in which to develop his art. But it was always a place where someone who simply enjoyed playing music would come to join others who shared his interest. The emphasis was on the enjoyment of a pursuit rather than the mastery of it. An annual sing-it-yourself gala at which all are invited to join in a rendition of Handel's Messiah is immensely popular. No one is disturbed that no recording contract is likely to be forthcoming.

In the past five to ten years, people have come to realize that San Francisco is a place to come to develop an art if only because it will be appreciated here. Museums have been well endowed and are well attended. A van Gogh exhibit in 1958 drew bigger crowds in San Francisco than in Los Angeles or New York, both cities with much larger populations.

The San Francisco Symphony performs to sell-out crowds in its new quarters in the Louise K. Davies Symphony Hall. The first municipal opera house in the country was here. Theater has been popular since the pioneer days. The San Francisco Ballet is the oldest in the country. In 1980 there were close to one hundred dance companies in the Bay Area. Some cultural events are sponsored in part by the city through a hotel tax fund. There is even an association of lawyers for the arts. (Of course, there are also lawyers here for almost any other cause you'd care to name.) The neighborhoods are dotted with small music, dance and theater companies which offer classical, improvisational and experimental pro-

ductions. A wide variety of ethnic music flourishes in San Francisco and you don't necessarily have to go seek out musical entertainment; street musicians will bring it to you.

San Franciscans like fun. Not everyone wants to work in an office. Some people prefer to earn their keep delivering messages dressed as singing egg plants. There are so many "silly services" available that a special directory was published to list them. Some of their best customers are the workers in the offices. The city which was willing to throw an international exposition at the drop of a hat still likes festive occasions. The annual Hallowe'en Ball is a celebration of the strange which draws crowds from throughout the city. San Franciscans still have a tolerance for characters and much will be forgiven a person who amuses them.

The place to which people once came to get rich is now a place where people accept smaller salaries than they could get elsewhere, in order to remain. It is a place where the quality of everyday life is important. While New Yorkers go to psychiatrists to help them adjust to society, Californians are more likely to look for a means to create a society which fits them. There are organizations which will offer to help you become whatever you want to be and, failing that, others that will convince you that what you are is what you ought to be. There is no conception of a mode of living so bizarre or far-fetched that it will not attract some adherents here. San Franciscans agree that "living well is the best revenge" but living well is a matter of knowing what is important to you. Lawrence Ferlinghetti said he came to San Francisco because it was the only place he could get good cheap wine.

Shakespeare and circuses are important to the vital, exuberant, cosmopolitan, often careless, and contradictory city on the bay. Is it, as Frank Norris said, "serene and indifferent to its fate"? Possibly. There has to have been something of that in the people who built their castles on the sand. Perhaps it is just that when the fog horns announce the arrival of the spring fog through the sunset strait into the Bay of St. Francis, it is too much to ask that people not believe this is a good place to live.

Even a city as vibrant as this has its quieter spots, where tourist and inhabitant can take time off to unwind from the hustle and bustle of everyday life.

It is difficult to imagine that the elegance and natural beauty of Golden Gate Park was nothing more than 1,000 acres of shifting sand dunes some 100 years ago. Today it boasts a host of recreational amenities and other attractions that draw the city dwellers to the area. Shown *right and below* are the Buddha statue and Japanese Tea Gardens. *Far right:* The ancient redwoods of Muir Woods National Monument soar skywards from the slopes of Mount Tamalpais.

Cathedral Grove

Facing page: Downtown San Francisco, seen from Mission Dolores Park, towers over the predominantly Latin area to the south.

Bright murals adorn walls and fences of the Mission District *above*, whilst flamboyant street characters *right and top centre* provide their own blend of colourful individuality to the everyday life of the city. *Facing page:* Union Square, seen from the St. Francis Hotel, stands at the heart of Downtown San Francisco and is a popular meeting point and lunchtime spot for office workers.

Instantly identifiable symbol of the city, the Golden Gate Bridge was completed in 1937 and elegantly spans the bay, linking San Francisco with the hills of Marin County to the north. The sparkling waters of the bay beneath provide ideal conditions for the fearless surfers, and the rocky coastline is a haven for the seals.

Crawling at a sedate 9½ miles per hour, the seemingly outmoded cable cars negotiate almost impossible gradients with an age-inspired confidence. *Facing page:* The imposing grandeur of the Sheraton-Palace Hotel's Garden Court.

Carefully tended exotic plants and flowers flourish in the humid atmosphere of the Victorian Conservatory in Golden Gate Park *above and top.* This ornate yet functional structure was manufactured in New York and then crated and shipped to the West Coast via Cape Horn. The still waters of an ornamental pool *right,* reflect the graceful shapes of an oriental-style pavilion, one of several to be seen in the park's Japanese Tea Garden.

The flashing lights and garish signs of Broadway proclaim the attractions of bars, clubs and restaurants that cater for every imaginable taste. Visitors flock to sample the entertainment that is reminiscent of the wildest days of the 'Gold Rush' and the fabled Barbary Coast, although to the San Franciscans, who have seen it all before, the area is little more than a tourist trap.

Being surrounded by water on three sides, it is hardly surprising that the sea plays such an important part in both the leisure and working lives of the people of San Francisco. Fisherman's Wharf, *left, top left and facing page,* is the landing point of the many local fishermen and, naturally enough, the area is famed for its excellent sea-food restaurants. Coit Tower, its shape designed to resemble a firehose nozzle, overlooks the Wharf from its lofty position on Telegraph Hill *above.*

Even as far back as 1839, it was apparent to the original city planners that scarcity of land would be a problem and, as a consequence, buildings were crammed together on the steep-sided hills. Today, this scarcity is even greater, meaning that new developments must look heavenward for space. The futuristic structures of the financial district grow ever higher. Few of these can rival the imaginative novelty of the pyramid-shaped Transamerica building, which seems to capture and draw the eye whenever it appears – almost a monument to the space age. *Facing page:* Seen from the air, Oakland Bridge provides a direct land link with the neighbouring city of Oakland. The massive steel structure pauses on Yerba Buena Island, pouring its traffic into a tunnel before continuing the f part of its journey.

Brightly painted weatherboarded properties that might offend the eye in other towns, fit perfectly into the youthfully exuberant character of this sun-kissed city. Unfortunately, not all such older buildings are as well preserved and many, having fallen into disrepair, are destined for demolition. Box-like houses litter the hilly landscape, jostling for space in one of San Francisco's early residential areas *facing page.*

Overleaf: **As night descends, boats and gull race landward across a shimmering sea, while morning brings with it a blanket of mist from which the waking city seems mystically to rise.**

Dusk brings with it sights familiar to any city dweller, as ant-like shop and office workers scurry home. San Francisco's busy Downtown district is almost a city within a city, each day attracting enormous crowds from all the outlying areas. *Above and facing page left:* **Powell St** climbs steeply to the historic heights of Nob Hill.

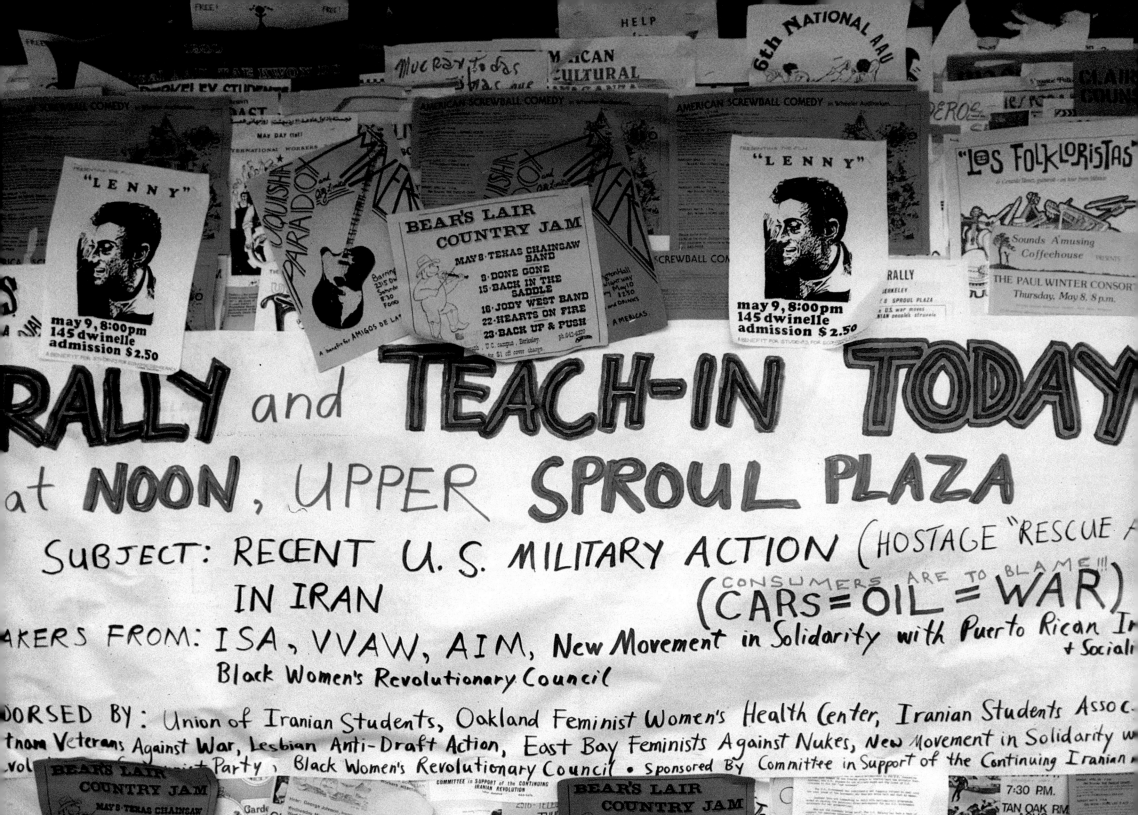

RALLY and TEACH-IN TODAY

at NOON, UPPER SPROUL PLAZA

SUBJECT: RECENT U.S. MILITARY ACTION (HOSTAGE "RESCUE A
IN IRAN (CONSUMERS ARE TO BLAME!!! CARS = OIL = WAR)

AKERS FROM: ISA, VVAW, AIM, New Movement in Solidarity with Puerto Rican I
+ Sociali
Black Women's Revolutionary Council

DORSED BY: Union of Iranian Students, Oakland Feminist Women's Health Center, Iranian Students Assoc.
tnam Veterans Against War, Lesbian Anti-Draft Action, East Bay Feminists Against Nukes, New Movement in Solidarity w
vol...ist Party, Black Women's Revolutionary Council • Sponsored By Committee in Support of the Continuing Iranian

Romanesque-style arches, exquisite stained glass windows and red-tiled roofs grace the fine buildings of Stanford University. Standing in over 8,000 acres of land at Palo Alto, it was founded in 1883 by railroad baron Leland Stanford. Oldest of all the campuses in California is the university at Berkeley *right*, almost a town in its own right.

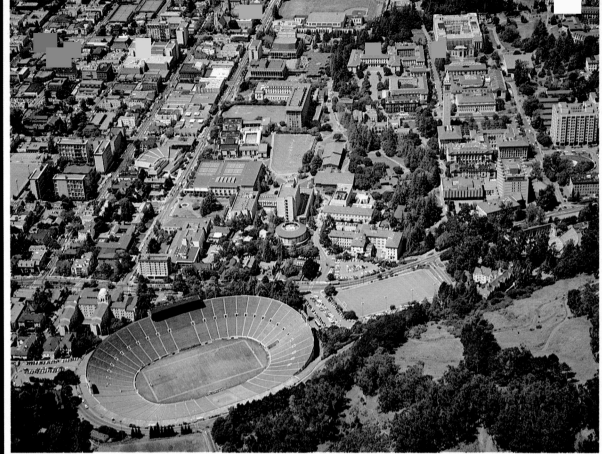

Spread over 24 blocks, San Francisco's Chinatown houses the largest Chinese community outside the Orient. As much an intrinsic part of the city as any other ethnic group, the Chinese originally came here in the heady days of the gold rush and, due to the persecution they were forced to endure, they formed a tight-knit protective community where their language, religion and customs have continued to flourish.

BUSINESS!
T MOVE!
LEASE NOW!

Grant Avenue, facing page a narrow but extremely busy thoroughfare, bisects Chinatown from north to south. Surrounded by a mass of Chinese faces, shops and even banks, it is easy to forget that one is in the heart of an American city. The dark shapes of the Oakland and Golden Gate Bridges *overleaf* tower over the twilit waters of the bay.

DONT WALK

Claiming to be the most crooked street in the world, Lombard snakes down from Leavenworth to Hyde, its well tended gardens providing a riot of colour. Coit Tower and the Transamerica Building *facing page* overlook a Fisherman's Wharf crammed with fishing boats at their moorings.

The cable cars of San Francisco *above* are a unique and surprisingly efficient means of transport. The first system, designed by Andrew Hallidie, was opened in 1873 and what remains has been designated a National Historic Landmark. The now disused prison island of Alcatraz stands in the middle of the bay *right*. Despite its proximity to the mainland, the unpredictable and vicious currents ensured its total security. *Top right:* The Transamerica building. *Facing page:* Oakland Bridge.

Now a tourist attraction, Alcatraz *top right* once housed the nation's most notorious criminals. *Top and above:* Oakland and Golden Gate bridges provide an essential link with the rest of California. *Right:* A forest of masts in Sausalito. *Facing page:* The marina.

Craft of all types and sizes ply the waters of this most magnificent of natural harbours.

Monolithic structures, some of singular beauty, others relatively plain, house the power-plants of many of the nation's most important financial and commercial institutions, making San Francisco the business capital of the West Coast. The tallest buildings offer superb panoramic views of the entire bay area.

Once proudly dominant, now dwarfed, this old building stands guard at the corner of Columbus and Pacific *far left. Left:* Unassuming weather-boarded houses line a narrow San Francisco street. Historic Fort Point *bottom left,* built in 1861 to guard the Golden Gate, now nestles inconspicuously under the south tower of the Golden Gate Bridge, its 127 cannon never fired in anger. *Bottom centre and below:* Immortalised in word, picture and song the non-polluting cable car is an integral part of San Francisco. *Facing page:* Age has not withered these fine old buildings.

Sleek from a distance but reassuringly massive close-to, the orange-painted pillar of the Golden Gate Bridge stands out against the soft evening sky *left*. San Francisco sunsets bring with them an impressive range of moods and colours *below and bottom*. A latticework of girders frames the silhouetted contours of the rocky headland beyond, *facing page*.

Cameos of city life: cable car and jogger frozen on the brow of a hill *left,* a policeman dispenses instant justice *above,* and passengers board an ascending cable car *top. Facing page:* Car tail-lights weave red patterns through the hilly streets.

At the foot of Powell Street *left*, a cable car is turned in readiness for its steady, snail-like ascent towards Nob Hill. *Below:* The tip of the Transamerica's spire points the way to future building development. A myriad lights shine from the office windows irradiating the city with their pale glow, *facing page*.
Overleaf: As offices close for the night, cars scurry homeward over Golden Gate Bridge.

Mouthwatering displays of fish and roasted duck hang tantalisingly in the food shop windows of Chinatown, tempting the passers-by to enter and make a purchase. At night, the many fine restaurants cater for an army of hungry customers.

Although not as elegant as its older brother, the Oakland Bridge, with its two tiers of traffic, is equally indispensable, the silver monster carrying a far greater volume of vehicles which would previously have had to cross the bay by ferry.

The frantic rush for gold and wealth brought people westward in their thousands. Today, that mineral wealth no longer exists, but still the people flock to this ever growing, most dynamic of the world's great cities.

Above: **Beyond the skyscrapers of the Downtown area, the houses of the East Bay communities spread across the Berkeley-Oakland hills.** *Facing page:* **The heart of the city glowing with man-made light.** *Overleaf left:* **Pavilion in the Japanese Tea Garden, Golden Gate Park.** *Overleaf right:* **Lone Mountain Campus, University of San Francisco.**

These pages: **Traditional architecture set against the ultramodern.** *Overleaf:* **Early residential areas in San Francisco consisted of small, detached rows of houses. These now form a pleasing contrast with the modern architectural styles.**

By the late 1860s, there were more than 15,000 Chinese laborers working on the east-west railroad. When it was completed – in Utah on May 10, 1869 – many of them decided to settle in San Francisco. Chinatown *these pages* was the result, although the original settlement was destroyed in the 1906 fire.

These pages: San Francisco is blessed by a large number of parks and gardens that exist for the people's relaxation and enjoyment. Golden Gate Park is perhaps the most elegant and was "primarily intended to provide the best practical means for healthful recreation for people of all classes." One of its most beautiful areas is the delightful Japanese Tea Garden *above,* which is most enjoyable when visited during cherry blossom time in April. John McLaren was the man responsible for transforming the park which, in 1887, he found as 730 acres of dunes and 270 acres of arable land. He liked to be known as "boss gardener" and made his first task the stabilizing of the dunes by planting the Australian tea tree, northern European beach grass and ice plant amongst them. He held the post of park superintendent for 59 years until his death in 1943. *Overleaf left:* City Hall, rebuilt after the 1906 earthquake. *Overleaf right:* The Golden Gate Bridge. John C. Fremont was the first man to use the term "Golden Gate". In his 1848 *Geographical Memoir of California* he wrote, "To this Gate I gave the name 'Chrysophlae' or Golden Gate, for the same reason the harbor of Byzantium was called 'Chrysoceras' or Golden Horn."

Above: **View of the city from Twin Peaks. Set between ocean and mountains, beneath the beneficent rays of the Californian sun, the city of San Francisco knows no equal.** *Facing page:* **Urban scene in the Market Street region.**

Top left: **The waterfront at Sausalito.** *Top right:* **The Palace of Fine Arts.** *Above:* **The Civic Center.** *Right:* **Fort Mason Marina.** *Facing page:* **View of Downtown from the Moscone Center.** *Overleaf:* **Night shots of the city from Telegraph Hill.**

Above: **View to the Downtown area, past children relaxing in the sunshine.** *Facing page:* **The San Francisco-Oakland Bay Bridge.**

Above: **Jack London Square and an unusual figure on the park bench.** *Facing page:* **The Civic Center.** *Overleaf:* **Victorian houses grace the older section of San Francisco.**

Left and top left: **The University of Southern California.** *Above:* **City Hall.** *Facing page:* **The Palace of Fine Arts, designed by Bernard Maybeck to resemble a Roman ruin. This stately building still remains from the Panama Pacific International Exposition of 1915, which acknowledged the role played by the opening of the Panama Canal in stimulating the growth of trade and industry in San Francisco.**

When the writer Rudyard Kipling came here in 1889 he said: "San Francisco is a mad city – inhabited for the most part by perfectly insane people." Times change, but perhaps Kipling's comment could be applied to any fast-living, 20th-century urban community.

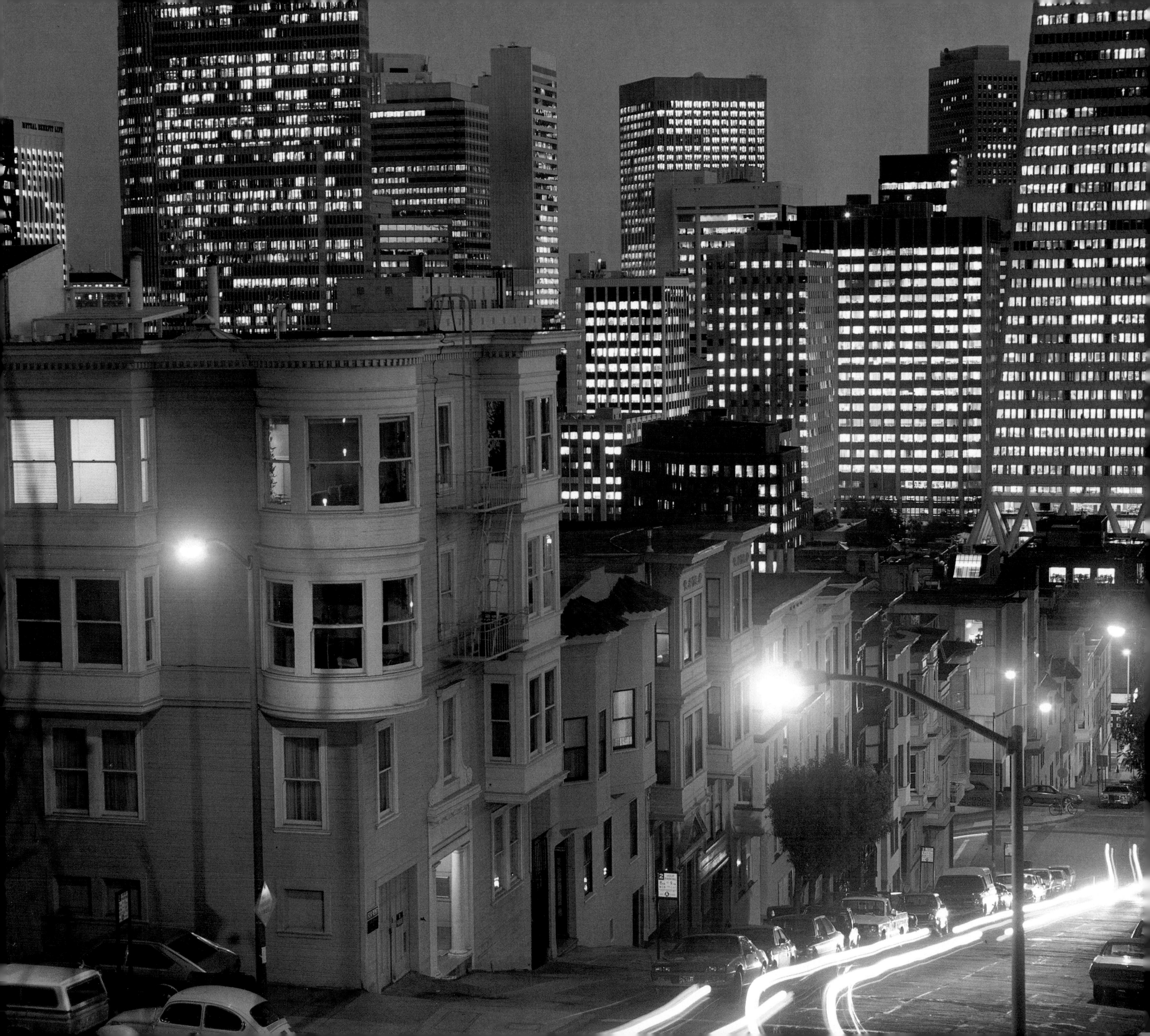

Above: **Bakers Beach, where half a mile of sandy beach is swept by the foaming surf.** *Facing page:* **A confusing latticework of cables above San Francisco's busy streets.**